HSBC  Insurance

Elephants in paper bags and steam in crates ...

Elephants in paper bags and steam in crates ...

A history of HSBC Insurance Brokers

Laurie Dennett and Stephanie Zarach

GRANTA EDITIONS

© Copyright HSBC Insurance Brokers Ltd. 2008

Published by Granta Editions, 25–27 High Street, Chesterton, Cambridge CB4 1ND, United Kingdom.
Granta Editions is a wholly owned subsidiary of Book Production Consultants Ltd.

ISBN 978 1 85757 092 2

A CIP catalogue record for this book is available from The British Library.

Designed by Peter Dolton.
Design, editorial and production in association with Book Production Consultants Ltd.,
25–27 High Street, Chesterton, Cambridge CB4 1ND, United Kingdom.

Printed by Norwich Colour Print Ltd, Drayton, Norwich, UK, on Regency Satin paper using vegetable oil-based inks. Made in Italy, the paper comprises 100% virgin fibre. Pulps used are elemental chlorine-free.

The FSC logo identifies products which contain wood from well-managed forests certified in accordance with the rules of the Forest Stewardship Council.

Mixed Sources
Product group from well-managed forests and other controlled sources
www.fsc.org Cert no. TT-COC-002425
© 1996 Forest Stewardship Council
FSC

Contents

Preface

Dear Reader

It is with great pleasure that I contribute the preface of this fine book. The HSBC Group is immensely proud of HSBC Insurance Brokers and its commercial antecedents stretching back to 1808. It is not possible to read the 200-year history of HSBC Insurance Brokers without being impressed by the entrepreneurialism and vigour of its management and owners.

Broking was born as a natural adjunct to the growth of British maritime power and the geography of the empire. The Lloyd's market and broking developed rapidly, innovatively and broadly. Indeed it was the productive relationship between Lloyd's underwriters and brokers that made the London market indispensable for many global businesses.

It is hard to imagine life in 1808. The Battle of Trafalgar had taken place three years earlier, culminating in victory over the French but at the cost of the death of Lord Nelson, someone for whom Lloyd's had huge respect. The population of London was less than one million people. Poverty was rife and the variety of jobs that the average man in the street would carry out was limited. The industrial revolution had yet to reveal the impact on employment of power-driven machinery. Until then much was crafted by hand in workshops in individuals' homes and sheds.

Yet amongst all this, in cities such as London and Bath, Georgian terraces with their distinctive houses had been designed and built by architects such as John Nash and Robert Adam. Interest in overseas travel, importing and exporting was growing.

The year 1808 saw the birth of Thomas Cook, who founded the famous Cook travel bureau. Also in that year anthracite coal was first burned as a fuel, and the original Covent Garden was destroyed by fire – along with most of its scenery, costumes and scripts. Beethoven conducted the premiere of his Fifth and Sixth Symphonies in Vienna, as well as performing his Fourth Piano Concerto.

Against this background the story of Antony Gibbs is indeed remarkable. Two hundred years on the authors have created a deft, fascinating business history, tracing the evolution of the company we see today from unusual beginnings.

We are fortunate to have had the skills and talents of two experienced authors who specialise in business histories. We owe them considerable gratitude in weaving together our business and client history. We are also most grateful to Tim Kemp and Charles Ledsam who managed the project and to those clients who contributed to the book.

Clive Bannister
Group Managing Director, Insurance
June 2008

Firm of purpose: the story of Antony Gibbs

A MAN CALLED ANTONY GIBBS

The origin of the oldest part of HSBC Insurance Brokers lies some 200 years in the past, with the firm established in 1808 by Antony Gibbs.

A full-length portrait of him still hangs in the City of London's Royal Exchange – where Lloyd's of London was based until the opening of its own building in 1928 – a tribute to him as a member of Lloyd's and the founder of a prosperous City firm. Even in the reproduction (see the page opposite) taken from an earlier history of the merchant banking firm Gibbs founded, the painting strikes the viewer as an attractive work. A fine-featured young man, confident of bearing, his wealth and refinement of taste evident in the satin and lace of his garments, gazes out of an idealised landscape and into the middle distance. It seems a conventional late 18th-century portrait of an English gentleman, born to prosperity and comfort.

But appearances, as everyone knows, can be deceptive, and the first impression conveyed by this painting is a case in point. For a start, although we know the subject's name, we also know that he owned no leafy acres to provide a Gainsborough-like setting for his portrait. His working life – for neither his circumstances nor his temperament permitted him to be a man of leisure – was anything but untroubled. He spent more than half his adult years abroad, and they were punctuated by enough of the adventures and near-disasters of a turbulent age to astonish us, even 200 years after the name of Antony Gibbs & Sons first graced a signboard in the City of London. In short, this charming painting is something of an illusion.

**Antony Gibbs of Topsham in Devon, painted
by Edward Patry, R.B.A., from a half-length
drawing by John Dowman, A.R.A.**

And yet…the clues to our subject's identity are there. He was born in 1756 at Topsham, a village on the river Exe a few miles downstream from Exeter. In the painting, we see the river glinting as it winds its way into the background, a broad channel that had made shipping and trade the mainstays of this part of Devon for centuries. Where the river bends, a city takes shape, shrouded in mist. Two pinnacled towers rise out of it: the towers of Exeter cathedral, landmarks in Antony Gibbs's day as in our own. Gibbs's painted figure stands in the same relation to the shrouded city as the town of Topsham in reality does to Exeter, so that in this sense he has indeed been depicted as standing "on his home ground". His resolute gaze westward now makes sense. That is the direction in which South America lies, and South America was the part of the world in which the firm of Antony Gibbs & Sons achieved its commercial success.

The painting, as may be apparent by now, was executed long after its subject's youth had passed, with the aim of commemorating him as the founder of a firm that had by then become great. The original enterprise, however, began very modestly. Antony Gibbs was one of the 11 children of George Gibbs, a surgeon. At 18, after some years at Exeter Grammar School, he was apprenticed to a Mr Brook, a merchant who exported locally made woollen cloth to Spain. At 22, Antony began exporting textiles to Spain and Italy on his own account, for a time taking a share in a woollen mill with one of his brothers. His father backed the expansion of the business and for a time it flourished, but in 1789, when he was 33, disaster struck and Antony became bankrupt. As Wilfred Maude's 1958 history of the firm puts it, despite being by now a married man with a family, Antony seems to have been "somewhat over sanguine and to have overtraded at a time when political conditions on the Continent rendered an exporter's business more than usually precarious". The fact that he struggled for the rest of his life to repay his creditors, leaving the sums still owing at his death as debts of honour upon his sons, says much about his character.

Antony now moved to Madrid, taking advantage of the experience he had gained in trading with Spain and his proficiency in the Spanish language to re-establish himself in the textile trade. Conditions, compared to those in England, were challenging, to say the least: roads – where they existed at all – were generally bad, and the country was swept by epidemics. The period following the French Revolution brought unsettled relations, then war, between France and Spain, which disrupted trade and travel. War drove Antony out of Spain altogether in 1797, and for a time he ran his business from Lisbon. In 1802 he tried to resume work in Spain, this time in Cadiz, but three years later, with Spain and England at war, he found himself an enemy alien, his goods at risk, and trade with England at a standstill. Retreating to Lisbon with his family, he left a quantity of goods valued at about £20,000* in the care of a friendly Spanish firm, to safeguard them from confiscation.

His problem now was how to realise this investment without falling foul of the Spanish authorities on land or the English on the high seas. Shipping them to one of the Spanish colonies of the New World and selling them there seemed to present a solution.

Antony made a clandestine journey to London – which was made more hair-raising still when his ship was captured by a privateer. This in turn was taken by an English ship, and Gibbs was eventually put ashore in his native Devon. With the help of family and diplomatic connections, he secured a licence that allowed the Spanish firm holding his goods to charter a vessel, the *Hermosa Mexicana*, and despatch them to Lima. The ship was then to take on a cargo of Peruvian produce and convey it to London.

Edward Lloyd's Coffee House was established late in the 17th century in Tower Street, London, and became a meeting place where merchants and shipowners discussed trade, shipping news and insurance matters.

* Please see Appendix 6 for relative monetary values.

News of the Battle of Trafalgar reaches
London. The 18 years during which Antony
Gibbs and his sons built up their business in
Spain and Portugal coincided with the tumult
of the Napoleonic and Peninsular Wars.
London Gazette, 1805

By 1808 Antony had accepted that his Spanish business was lost. The prudent
course, if he were to leave anything to his sons, was to operate from the City of
London. His decision was made easier by an invitation to become one of four
Commissioners dealing with Portuguese property in England, following the invasion

of Portugal by the French. The post was modestly and irregularly paid, but it brought him into contact with City banking, broking, shipping and insurance circles. It also gave his sons first-hand experience of commercial life.

In September 1808 Antony opened an office in Sherborne Lane, just off Lombard Street, taking his elder son Henry into partnership. The firm was called Antony Gibbs & Son (but when William, the younger, became a partner in 1813, the name was altered to Antony Gibbs & Sons, and remained so until 1948). At almost the same time Antony re-opened an office in Cadiz under the name of Antony Gibbs, Son & Branscombe, the last-named being his former clerk. This was a far-sighted measure, since Cadiz was the main port for trade with the Spanish overseas territories and, unlike the rest of the country, had not been overrun by the French. A further step involved setting up an office in the newly acquired British possession, Gibraltar, to send more shipments of Spanish goods to South America. This office lasted until 1833.

Antony was thus able to capitalise on the experience and goodwill built up during the 18 years when he had been a member of the business communities of Madrid, Cadiz and Lisbon. He had acted as agent in the Iberian peninsula for the leading English textile exporters, and it would seem that from the firm's beginnings he was asked to arrange insurance for clients' goods. One of his brothers, George, was also involved in seaborne trade, along with Charles Bright, a Melbourne merchant, as a founding partner of Gibbs, Bright & Co. This partnership had offices in Bristol and Liverpool, and several agencies in the Caribbean. Antony's firm took on the sale of the West Indian produce imported by Gibbs, Bright and in other ways worked closely with it. In addition, the contacts in Peru made through the sale of goods carried by the *Hermosa Mexicana* provided the basis for continuing trade with Peru and later, with Chile.

S.S. *Great Britain* flying the Gibbs, Bright pennant.

Facing Page:
Cadiz harbour. In the 18th century, the Spanish government transferred its very considerable trading activities with Spanish America from its port at Seville to Cadiz, which had better access to the Atlantic. In consequence, Cadiz became one of Spain's most cosmopolitan cities and an ideal place for Antony Gibbs to have an office.

Drawn by Lieut Col. Batty.   Engraved by E. Finden.

Gibbs sails full circle

When Isambard Kingdom Brunel, the great 19th-century engineer, was in the employ of the Great Western Railway Co. as head engineer, he persuaded Great Western Railway to build one large, fast ship both to compete in the race to deliver mail and to take advantage of the growing demand of passengers to visit America.

The new ship, the S.S. *Great Britain*, was planned as a conventional steamer with paddle wheels but Brunel had more ambitious ideas. The final design of this, the first iron-hulled ship ever, was altered to incorporate a new screw type six-bladed propeller which was operated by

a steam engine delivering a service speed of 9 knots. She carried six masts and sails in case the steam engine malfunctioned. The vessel was officially launched on 19 July 1843. It took another two years to fit her out with the most luxurious accommodation that had ever put to sea: she was the world's largest ship, being 100 feet longer than her nearest rivals, and with 130 crew she still had cabins enough for 252 passengers.

Brunel's ship set out on her maiden voyage from Liverpool on 26 July 1845, arriving in New York just 14 days later, the first iron-hulled propeller-driven vessel ever to cross the Atlantic. However despite such a hopeful start, a serious mishap occurred in the following year, when the ship ran aground on the rocky coast of Ireland at Dundrum Bay and destroyed her engines. She remained stranded for a year until there was a tide high enough to float her off, but by this time Great Western Railway had incurred unsustainable losses and the ship was sold to Gibbs, Bright & Co. for £18,000 in 1850. The Gibbs in this instance was

George, brother of Antony of Antony Gibbs & Sons fame; the plan was to use the ship to transport increasing numbers of emigrants from Britain to Australia.

For this purpose, the S.S. *Great Britain* was refitted with new, slightly less powerful engines and she was re-rigged. Her cabins were also refitted, offering accommodation for 750 passengers in

Brunel's ship set out on her maiden voyage from Liverpool on 26 July 1845, arriving in New York 14 days later.

three classes. She set out on her first voyage from Liverpool to Melbourne on 21 August 1852 and, with a refuelling stop at St Helena, took 120 days to complete the round trip. The ship operated the Australian run for the next three years.

The S.S. *Great Britain* was requisitioned for military purposes during the Crimean War in 1855–56 and used as a troop carrier. She was refitted again when she returned to commercial service, and worked the Australian run for the next 20 years for the Liverpool & Australian Navigation Co., part of the Gibbs, Bright enterprise. She was acquired by Antony Gibbs & Sons, which had taken over the failing Gibbs, Bright & Co. in 1882, and converted to a three-mast windjammer carrying Welsh coal and wheat to San Francisco around Cape Horn. But in 1885 she was forced to seek refuge at Port Stanley in the Falkland Islands after being badly damaged in a storm off Cape Horn. The repairs required proved too expensive for Antony Gibbs and so the company sold her to the Falklands Trading Company as a floating coal and wool storage hulk. After such a bright and pioneering beginning, the S.S. *Great*

Britain, by now over 40 years old, endured the ignominy of this static life for an astonishing 50 years before being scuttled off the Falkland Islands at Sparrow Cove on 12 April 1937, six years short of her hundredth birthday.

For many a ship this would have been the end of the line, but a recovery group was formed in 1968 and raised sufficient money to refloat her and bring her home on 12 April 1970. She was brought back to Bristol, to the very dock from which she had emerged as a newbuilding 130 years before. She was restored to her former glory over the next 35 years, utilising new technology to help preserve her from the elements. Now a museum in Bristol docks, the ship has won 14 awards, including several for excellence in restoration and conservation.

The Next Generation

Antony, alas, did not live to see these interests mature. He died in 1815 at the early age of 59, worn out by exertion. Henry and William Gibbs took a cousin, Charles Crawley, into the partnership in 1820, but in practice, because of Henry's poor health, it was William Gibbs who now assumed the leading role. He had worked closely with his father in Spain, and was thoroughly at home and respected in Spanish commercial circles.

This was a propitious time to be engaged in trade with South America. Peru gained its independence from Spain in 1818, Chile in 1820, and Argentina in 1823. While the former colonies possessed enormous mineral wealth, they lacked the

William Gibbs, Antony's elder son, was "Prior" or head of the firm from 1842 to 1875. He was one of Victorian England's great philanthropists.

Antony Gibbs & Sons' office from 1826 to 1850 was located at 47 Lime Street in the City of London and known as the "Compting House".

infrastructure necessary to develop it. Investment and expertise were badly needed to replace the capital lost through the departure of the Spanish elite. The resources that flowed first into this vacuum were largely British. Antony Gibbs & Sons was one of the earliest British firms to establish itself in South America, and would become one of the most important. Initially, it opened offices in Lima, Peru, in 1822, and in the Chilean towns of Valparaiso and Santiago in 1826. An "office" really meant a kind of depot, with wharves for the loading of cargo vessels and warehouses for the safe storage of goods.

The London headquarters, or "compting house", soon outgrew its premises in Sherborne Lane and moved, first to Great Winchester Street, then to 47 Lime Street, a Jacobean mansion with very fine panelling and ceilings. (When this building was eventually demolished, parts of it were given to the Victoria and Albert Museum.) In 1850 the firm moved to 22 Bishopsgate, where it would remain for well over a century. This handsome building dated from about 1750 and boasted some ornate 18th-century interiors. The premises came to occupy several adjacent houses as these came up for sale and as the number of employees steadily increased – from 19 in 1846 to 50 by 1860.

It was at the Lime Street office that discussions took place between the Gibbs brothers and representatives of Gibbs, Bright that resulted in the incorporation in 1835 of the first railway line between London and Bristol, the Great Western Railway. Gibbs, Bright was also the loading agent of the first steamer to cross the Atlantic, Isambard Kingdom Brunel's *Great Western*. Gibbs, Bright had built up a sizeable mercantile business in Australia, and in 1850 purchased the *Great Britain*, the biggest ship yet built, to operate a passenger service between Liverpool and Melbourne. Later the service was extended to Brisbane, Sydney, Adelaide and Perth.

After years of ill-health, the founder's elder son, Henry Gibbs, died in 1842.

Keble College, Oxford, was commissioned and paid for by William Gibbs, who engaged his friend William Butterfield, one of the foremost architects of the Gothic Revival, to design it.

William Gibbs and Charles Crawley were both devout Anglicans who supported the Oxford Movement, and Crawley eventually left the Gibbs firm to join John Henry Newman's circle at Littlemore. William remained the senior partner, or "Prior" – a title unique to Antony Gibbs & Sons that revealed William's view of it as a community, with himself at its head and definite ideals – until his death in 1875. In later life he became a notable philanthropist, endowing a host of churches and commissioning the building of Keble College, Oxford. He also purchased a Georgian mansion in the West Country called Tyntes Place, and over many years extended it until, as Tyntesfield, it became a magnificent example of Gothic Revival architecture and decoration.

Henry's son, Henry Hucks Gibbs, entered the firm in a junior position in 1843 and

Tyntesfield, the magnificent house created by William Gibbs around the original, more modest dwelling known as Tyntes Place. It is now a National Trust property.

was made a partner in 1848. He would supply a remarkable degree of stability and continuity, serving until his death in 1907. As a director of the Bank of England, then as its governor (1875–77), and as M.P. for the City of London in 1891–92, he also brought the firm a good deal of prestige. He was created Baron Aldenham in 1897. The terms of office of William Gibbs and Henry Hucks Gibbs coincided with a dramatic rise in the firm's prosperity and reputation.

Guano and Growth

Until nearly the middle of the 19th century, the business of Antony Gibbs & Sons remained basically what it had always been: the export of English textiles to Spain and South America on commission, sometimes assisting clients by acting as bankers and placing the insurances of ships and cargoes. Both Gibbs brothers were members of Lloyd's, and Henry was a director of the London Assurance Corporation. The Lima office was an agency for Lloyd's and for the London and Glasgow Insurance Associations from 1821, and was active in both marine and non-marine insurance.

In 1841, however, the office in Lima announced something new: it was about to sign a contract with the governments of Peru and Bolivia for the purchase of a consignment of guano, or sea-bird droppings. This substance, used since ancient times as a fertiliser by the local people, was found in great abundance in Tarapacá province and on several off-shore islands. The Peruvian government wished to exploit it, and as sole owner consigned the right to export it to two British firms with which trusting relationships had developed. One was Antony Gibbs & Sons, whose efforts proved so profitable that from 1848 it was granted a monopoly over the trade. By then, sales of guano were providing over two-thirds of Peru's state revenue.

The harbour at Callao, Peru, in about 1860.
Exports of guano were at their height, and
Antony Gibbs & Sons at its most prosperous.

The Gibbs representatives in South America understood that guano was a most effective fertilising agent, but at the time of the first contract it was as yet an unknown quantity in Britain. Until the 1840s, apart from the natural fertilisers available in every barnyard, the standard addition to agricultural soils was bones, which were high in phosphates, low in nitrogen, and slow-acting because they took time to break down and release their nutrients. These characteristics limited the range of soils to which they could be applied (they were not very suitable for clay, for example). Guano, on the other hand, was rich in nitrogen as well as phosphates, and much more soluble. It was therefore likely to be more effective over a wider range of soils and crops: a good all-purpose manure that was also lighter and easier to transport.

The London office realised that the virtues of guano would have to be promoted to the British farmer, and produced such publications as *Guano: Its Analysis and Effects; Illustrated by the Latest Experiments* (1843) to help this process along. The

Facing Page:
Guano, or sea-bird droppings, was regarded with suspicion by British farmers when first recommended as a fertiliser. By 1850, however, supply could barely keep up with demand.

results achieved by a few big landowners who could afford to experiment helped to break down the initial suspicions of farmers towards the new material. Once its benefits became known, demand increased sharply. Amounts imported by Antony Gibbs & Sons went from 22,500 tons in 1846 to 199,700 tons in 1851. What this meant in financial terms can be roughly estimated, since the price per ton until 1854 was £9 5s, of which the Peruvian government received about £4. Even after paying the high cost of shipping its consignments of guano to Britain, Antony Gibbs & Sons stood to make excellent profits.

The height of the firm's involvement with the Peruvian guano trade came during the 1850s, with imports reaching 211,000 tons in 1856. By the late 1850s, supplies of guano for the British market were beginning to be less predictable. Some of the largest deposits were almost dug out, and there were occasional shortages of the manpower needed to get the product to the ships and load it. Two other factors played a part in the gradual slackening of the trade. First, strong competitors to guano had emerged, including nitrate of soda and – thanks to recent advances in agricultural chemistry – the cheaper superphosphate fertilisers. Secondly, there was the determination of the Peruvian government to capitalise on the demand for guano by raising the price per ton to £12, then to £13 – a price that British farmers were unwilling to pay, especially when cheaper alternatives were available. The Gibbs Lima office sought to temper the government's demands, since forcing down the demand for guano by raising its price was no more in Peru's long-term interest than it was in the firm's, but to no avail. The amount of guano imported into Britain began to exceed sales, so that in the years 1857 and 1858 there was a surplus of some 330,000 tons. As the *Journal of Agriculture* commented, "the Peruvians have done more injury to the sale of their guano than their worst enemies could have wished for". Earnings from guano sales were halved between the late 1850s and the late 1870s.

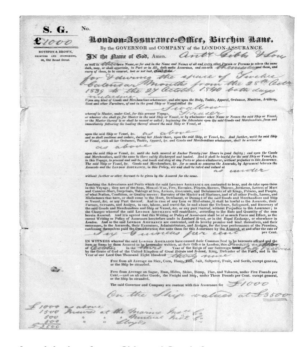

An original proforma Ship and Goods form dated 1839, issued to Captain Fraser in respect of insurance for a 12 month period which covered the vessel, contents and personal effects. The documents itemise the value and percentage covered by each of the insurers and Lloyd's underwriters and the calculated premium.

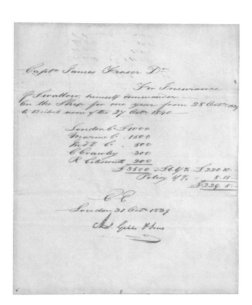

The covering letter, dated February 1840, enclosed with the SG form and details of charges goes on to report in the last paragraph the sudden loss of the *Tyrian* and five crew members off Gravesend, one of whom was known personally to Captain Fraser.

Antony Gibbs & Sons enjoyed a monopoly of the Peruvian guano trade until 1861, and continued to participate in it after that date, despite the difficulties. Guano was, after all, a renewable resource, and there was always a market for it in Britain even if peak demand had passed. The Lima office was closed in 1880, just before the outbreak of a territorial war between Chile on one hand and Peru and Bolivia on the other. Following Chile's defeat of Peru and Bolivia, the Chilean government asked the help of Antony Gibbs & Sons in realising the sale of a large quantity of guano captured from Peru. In this the firm's experience was invaluable, and the prior financial arrangements made by the Peruvian government with various European bond-holders were amicably settled.

Samuel Plimsoll, and a Debt to Antony Gibbs & Sons

An unfortunate adjunct to the growth of Britain's seaborne trade was the high inci-dence of ships that foundered through overloading. There was every incentive for ship-owners and masters to get maximum service for minimum expenditure. There was no legislation to prevent ships in poor condition being sent to sea. Worse still, masters often had a part interest in the cargo. Ill-maintained ships could be loaded to the gun-wales, and even a moderate storm could spell disaster. The loss of a ship and cargo was a matter for the insurers in London, but there was no compensation for loss of life.

Such instances had become all too common by the time Samuel Plimsoll took up the cause of the seamen whose lives were put at risk through irresponsibility and greed. As M.P. for Derby from 1868, he was able to prompt a Royal Commission on the question of load-lines and safety at sea in 1873. Despite being barred from the Commons for a time for his attacks on the shipowning interest, Plimsoll triumphed with the passing of the Merchant Shipping Act of 1876.

One of Plimsoll's tactics in his long battle was to publish his findings as a book entitled *Our Seamen*. It scandalised the nation, but it also made public the debt the campaign owed to Antony Gibbs & Sons. As a letter to Plimsoll reproduced in the book explained, the firm engaged hundreds of ships each year in the course of its export of guano from Peru. At first it hired the ships it needed, without enquiring too closely into their condition or the way the masters loaded them. Over time, the losses occasioned by such a casual approach moved the Gibbs agent at Lima, a Mr Stubbs, to take the initiative. He began to enforce the inspection, before and after loading, of any ship engaged by the firm, and to issue a certificate of fitness to sail. The mark-ing of a load-line on the hull became obligatory. From the time these regulations were imposed, there were no further losses of ships through poor condition or overloading.

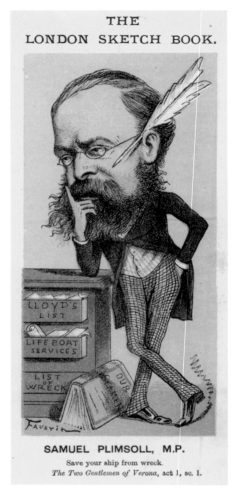

THE
LONDON SKETCH BOOK.

SAMUEL PLIMSOLL, M.P.
Save your ship from wreck.
The Two Gentlemen of Verona, act 1, sc. 1.

Samuel Plimsoll, M.P., took up the cause of
seamen whose lives were endangered by the
practice of overloading ships.

Merchant to Merchant Banker

The character of trans-Atlantic trade was now changing rapidly. The speed of the steamship and the telegraph heightened competition, which in turn reduced the commission that could be made on cargoes. The ambitions of governments in the South American countries where Antony Gibbs & Sons traded also meant that pressure for a greater national share of the profits on the sale of raw materials was likely to increase. It became clear that reliance on the prosperity generated by sales of a single commodity, such as guano, was unwise, and consequently the building up of other services, mainly to private and commercial clients, became a priority.

From its beginnings, the firm had acted as banker to some of its Spanish clients, which in time came to include members of the aristocracy. Once established in the City of London, it did the same for individual clients there. Besides the loans and the administration of funds that this entailed, related activities such as holding deposits against goods, the collection of dividends, and the custody, purchase and sale of securities evolved naturally out of these relationships of trust. Over the course of the century the firm's profile as a merchant bank developed, particularly in the area of acceptance credits, and it was as an accepting house, and eventually as a member of the Accepting Houses Committee, that it became best known.

Its predominant commercial activity, however, was coming to be the export of nitrates from Chile. The firm's first interest in this material was as a shareholder in the nitrate works at Antofagasta, then located in territory claimed by Bolivia. A three-way border dispute, followed by the war (mentioned above) in 1880 in which Peru's Tarapacá province and its rich nitrate fields was annexed by the victorious Chile, paved the way for the more extensive production of nitrate of soda. By now nitrates posed strong competition to guano, and the growing market for it offset to

The sailors' friend

Samuel Plimsoll's name became famous when the load lines marked on the side of ships were named after him. Today we take these lines for granted as being part of a ship's safety measures, but unscrupulous 19th-century shipowners did all they could to avoid them.

Plimsoll was not the first to contend that load lines should be used to ensure that vessels could not be overloaded. It is believed that lines date back to ancient Crete, when vessels were supposed to pass loading inspections before they sailed. The Romans also included such a regulation in their maritime rules, as did the Venetians later on.

Lloyd's Register introduced loading recommendations in 1835 after talks with shipowners, shippers and underwriters, but the lines were not compulsory and some shipowners were apt to ignore them. Overloaded ships commonly foundered with great loss of life and with considerable cost to their insurers.

Plimsoll, elected Liberal Member of Parliament for Derby in 1868, battled hard to have a Bill passed which would delineate load lines beyond which ships would be unsafe. The opposition he faced from the shipowning interest was balanced by support from insurers and the well-respected firm of Antony Gibbs & Sons. In Plimsoll's book on the subject, entitled *Our Seamen*, published in 1872, he quoted verbatim a letter dated 17 February 1871 which he had received from one Mr G Reid, a surveyor at Callao working under Mr Stubbs, who was the head of Antony Gibbs's offices in Lima, Peru.

Reid described a contract which the firm agreed with the Peruvian government to charter and load ships with guano from the Chincha Islands. The trade was considerable, involving three or four hundred ships which left the islands each year, destined for ports all over the world. Initially, the ships

were neither inspected nor surveyed before or after loading, the level of cargo being decided upon by the masters. The consequence of the resulting overloading was huge losses of life, of cargo and the ships themselves "so much so that hardly three days would pass without

The mark, which became known as the Plimsoll Line, was originally a circle with a horizontal line through it.

A Royal Commission was set up in 1873 to consider whether the Board of Trade should be empowered to make a loading mark on all ships.

hearing of some accident or loss, through the ships being allowed to overload and proceed to sea in an unlawful condition".

Mr Stubbs, who was responsible for chartering the ships to transport the guano, finally ordered that all ships used by Antony Gibbs for the guano trade must be surveyed before loading and inspected afterwards. A certificate would then be issued stating the condition of the ship and detailing any repairs required. It would also stipulate the height of the line on the ship's side which would represent its limit of loading. Copies of this certificate were given to the office and to the master of the ship. Once the ship was loaded it was inspected again, whereupon another certificate was issued if it was deemed seaworthy. The Customs House could only clear the ship to go to sea if the master could provide this last certificate.

Mr Reid said that soon "after the above rules were enforced a sudden and wonderful improvement took place, and during the four years I was surveyor afterwards not one ship foundered at sea, and only about two or three percent met with accidents".

A Royal Commission was set up in 1873 to consider whether the Board of Trade should be empowered to make a loading mark on all ships, and a bill was introduced to the House of Commons – but without success. Finally, such was Plimsoll's popular support that the British government under the prime minister Benjamin Disraeli was forced to act: the Merchant Shipping Act 1876 finally gave stringent powers to the Board of Trade to inspect a ship and make a mark beyond which the ship could not be loaded, to ensure that it retained sufficient buoyancy for its voyage. The mark, which became known as the Plimsoll Line, was originally a circle with a horizontal line through it.

Although the load-line was made compulsory in 1876, its positioning was not fixed by law until 1894. In 1906 ships visiting British ports had to be marked with a line, and finally the 1930 Load Line Convention signified international agreement for the universal application of load-line regulations. Today such a line is considered the norm.

WILLS'S CIGARETTES.

THE PLIMSOLL MARK.

some degree the decline in guano's popularity. Following the closure of the Gibbs' Lima office, a new base was set up at Iquique in Chile in 1881. The firm began to manufacture nitrate of soda at a number of factories in Tarapacá province, but apart from a few shipments it left the actual export and distribution of the product to others.

Nitrate and New Ventures

The important role of nitrates in the manufacture of explosives, as well as its use as a fertiliser, meant that firms from other countries soon obtained manufacturing concessions. Re-armament among the European powers and a strong demand for nitrates to serve the munitions industries, particularly those of Britain, Germany and France, characterised the latter part of the century. Nitrates became Chile's most important export, others being iodine, which could be made very cheaply as a by-product of nitrates, and copper. The export duties on nitrates and the general prosperity of the industry became mainstays of the Chilean economy.

Of the foreign firms operating in Chile, Antony Gibbs & Sons was the most important. The Chilean government came to rely on its experience with both nitrates and iodine, and on its connections in the wider commercial sphere. Proof of this was demonstrated when the firm became the London agent for the Chilean state railway when this was being built. The Gibbs' London office was also entrusted with the sale of four warships – two belonging to Chile and two to Argentina – being built in Europe and only partially paid for, when in 1902 these countries decided to halt the "arms race" they had been pursuing and ask for the firm's help in resolving their disagreements. Working closely with the British government, the firm arranged the

Munitions factory during the First World War.
Thanks to its dominant position in the
international nitrate trade, Antony Gibbs &
Sons was commissioned by the British
government to purchase, ship and finance
the nitrate requirements for wartime
munitions.

sale of two of the ships to Japan, then persuaded H.M. Government to buy the other
two to pre-empt their possible purchase by Russia.

A similar, but more serious, instance of the trust enjoyed by Antony Gibbs &
Sons in nitrate-producing circles arose in 1907, when large shipments of nitrates
were *en route* to Europe unsold. The London office organised and financed the formation of a nitrate pool for all the distributors, to avoid the need for quick sales and
the consequent fall in prices, which would have damaged Chile's economy. In the
course of arranging the pool, the firm acquired the French and Belgian agencies of
Schintz & Co. of Liverpool, another large nitrate concern. In 1910 an agreement
with the Hamburg firm of Hugo Wirtz brought access to the German market. Finally,
following the establishment in 1912 of Antony Gibbs & Co. Inc., New York, the firm
gained entry to the American market through an agreement with selling agents
H.J. Baker & Bros. in 1913.

The Great War and After

Much of this trade was, of course, disrupted by the outbreak of war in August 1914. In view of the firm's experience of the nitrate business on both sides of the Atlantic, the British government requested that it assume the task of filling the nation's requirements for nitrates for munitions. This included the financing, purchasing and shipping of the material, arranging and sometimes building the storage for it, and delivering it to the munitions factories. The firm also financed and purchased vast quantities – some 3,800,000 tons in all – of nitrates for the Allies, until in December 1917 a Nitrate of Soda Executive was set up jointly by the Allied countries themselves to co-ordinate supplies. All this handling of nitrates was carried out by the firm's Nitrate department, headed by George Korn. The Hon. Herbert Gibbs, who served through the war as liaison between the firm and the government, was awarded a peerage in 1923 in recognition of the wartime service rendered to the nation by Antony Gibbs & Sons – more often than not, without fee.

Nitrates remained a major concern, in both senses of the word, in the immediate post-war period and through the 1920s. Vast existing stocks of nitrates awaiting sale on one hand and overproduction on the other were bad enough, but now Chile's dominance as a source was being challenged. In response to the wartime blockade, Germany had herself begun to produce the 800,000 tons per year she required for armaments. With the return of peace, this independent national capacity was directed to the production of fertilisers. Further competition came from huge American companies such as Du Pont and Guggenheim, which set up offices in Chile and devised cheaper methods. The existing native and European producers sought protection by forming themselves into an association, but prices were out of line with what the American producers could offer, and the situation rapidly deteriorated.

**Bateman cartoon:
Distinguished visitor who signs the loss book
by mistake**

It was in this context that in 1921 Antony Gibbs & Sons was once again asked to form a pool and act as its agent. The background has been comprehensively set out by Wilfred Maude in his 1958 history of the firm; it is enough to say here that 20 producers were involved, that together they contributed around a million tons to the pool, and that about a third of this belonged to Antony Gibbs & Sons. Sales of the firm's holding eventually realised about £13 million of the £20 million it had been worth in better days, so that, like the rest of the nitrate community, the firm suffered severe losses over the decade. Until this time the financing of nitrate business had been arranged by the firm, but now, to contain the damage, a Chilean subsidiary (Cia Exportadora de Salitre de Chile, with a capital of £200,000) was formed to act as exporters and dealers, to be financed by credits granted by the firm and several other City merchant banks.

Losses on such a scale naturally implied a certain amount of belt-tightening on the part of the firm. General acceptance business was reduced, but it was fortunate that a new involvement arose that offset the disappointing situation of nitrates. This was the importation of hardwood timber from Australia, initially through a London-based agent but later via a company formed by Gibbs, Bright called Hardwoods (Australia) Proprietory Limited. The firm also became the London agent of the Western Australian State Sawmills, which produced plywood.

The nitrate market did not improve as the 1920s went on; rather, the export duties imposed by Chile acted as an additional deterrent to sales. In 1928 Antony Gibbs & Sons and three other exporters formed another new company to act as buyers, exporters and dealers in nitrates in Europe and Egypt: the Chilean Nitrate of Soda Distributors Limited. It enjoyed a successful few years until, in 1930, the Chilean government suddenly nationalised the nitrate and iodine industries. A state-owned company, the initials of which (COSACH) supplied the name by which it came to be known, took over all the producers and shipping companies, and nitrates and iodine became government monopolies. In 1932, all exports were assigned to the newly created Corporación de Ventas de Salitre y Yodo de Chile. The London-based Nitrate Corporation of Chile was set up to handle nitrate sales and distribution in Europe and Egypt. Antony Gibbs & Sons' long involvement in the production, export and sale of nitrates came to an end, though it continued to act as agent for the sale in Europe of Chilean iodine. It also played an essential part in securing credits for COSACH and subsequent ventures, co-ordinating the terms under which 23 London bankers and accepting houses were prepared to grant credits for £3 million for the Nitrate Corporation of Chile.

Branching out in Insurance

The firm's international seaborne trade generated a great deal of insurance business, not only of cargoes and ships, but of all the supporting infrastructure of the various ports and ground transport. Some of this was placed directly with the insurers, and some through a series of Lloyd's brokers. Marine insurance was usually placed with the Union Insurance Society of Canton, while almost all the non-marine insurance was placed with the Guardian Assurance, or with the London Assurance (of which both the second Lord Aldenham and the third became directors). The date by which the firm had a separate insurance department is uncertain, but by 1900 such a department was occupying the first floor of 22 Bishopsgate.

In 1920, a manager made a novel suggestion to the partners: that the Insurance department seek admission to Lloyd's as brokers, arranging any business that came its way by direct negotiation with the underwriters. This was done, so that from 1921 the department became brokers at Lloyd's with the manager in question, a Mr Hurndall, in charge. Much of the insurance placed was, of course, related to the trade in nitrates.

With the nationalisation of that industry in 1930, and the firm's appointment as joint brokers (with Sedgwick Collins & Co. Ltd and Lambert Bros. (Insurance) Ltd) to the Nitrate Corporation of Chile Ltd in London, it was decided to establish a separate insurance broking company, and in 1931 Antony Gibbs & Sons (Insurance) Ltd was formed. For a time, G.H. Booker of the Liverpool-based Booker McConnell

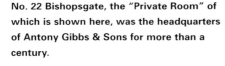

No. 22 Bishopsgate, the "Private Room" of which is shown here, was the headquarters of Antony Gibbs & Sons for more than a century.

Steamship Company had an interest in the new company, but from 1934 it was a wholly owned subsidiary of Antony Gibbs & Sons.

This was the beginning of a trend during the 1930s by which the firm organised some of the services it provided into separate entities, so as to rationalise its departmental and accounting structure. Antony Gibbs & Sons (Nominees) Ltd was formed as a holding company for clients' securities in 1932, while in 1935 the Anton Trust Co. was established to underwrite new issues and identify promising start-ups, along the lines suggested by the Macmillan Report of 1931.

A further foray into the Lloyd's market came on 1 January 1937, when six "Names" established a syndicate under the aegis of Antony Gibbs & Sons (Insurance) Ltd to write marine and non-marine insurance. The syndicate was very active, and grew in numbers until the outbreak of war in 1939. The higher premiums payable due to War Risk meant that income continued to rise during the war. After it, both income and the number of Names grew apace, along with the amount of marine, non-marine and aviation insurance needed in a recovering world. By 1956 there were four syndicates with a total of 94 Names.

While the City-based subsidiary placed a good deal of U.K. business, it was to be expected that the nature of Antony Gibbs & Sons as an international trading company would result in a high proportion of insurance originating overseas. (One of the more salutary transactions of this type came during the war, when the insurance subsidiary brokered the construction risk of Tasmania's highly experimental Hobart Bridge. When a gale damaged the bridge before completion, the underwriters settled for the entire sum insured.) It was also to be expected that the experience gained with one client, one class of insurance or one geographical area would lead to introductions and further business. So it was after the war, when contacts revived along with the economies of the industrialised world. Since the 1930s Antony Gibbs & Co.

Inc. in the United States had acted as buying and shipping agents for Campbell Bros. & Carter, which had a large clientele in South Africa and the Rhodesias. Their insurance requirements, placed with Antony Gibbs & Sons (Insurance) Ltd after the war, prompted the London office to explore the more general insurance possibilities in that developing region. As a result, Gibbs Foley & Co. (Pty), based in Johannesburg, was founded in 1948, and Gibbs & Co. (Central Africa) (Pty) Ltd, with an office in what was then Salisbury, in 1950, though subsequently both subsidiaries were absorbed into the parent company.

Similarly, the earlier connection with G.H. Booker led to the appointment of Antony Gibbs & Sons (Insurance) Ltd as brokers to Booker McConnell, which had large shipping and sugar interests in the Caribbean. The visits necessary to service this account gave the staff concerned a valuable knowledge of local conditions and, as an earlier account of this period put it, "it followed naturally that opportunities should be sought for extending the business". Agencies were established on the major islands in the West Indies, and in (as it then was) British Honduras, to produce an insurance network that was "both substantial and varied, in the conduct of which the Company has first-hand local knowledge".

From the City Stage to the World Stage

Antony Gibbs & Sons survived the war years, 1939 to 1945, relatively unscathed, though individual outposts around the world were forced to weather extremely trying times. In Britain, the rigours of wartime lasted well past the Armistice, necessitating all manner of adaptations. Some of these were occasioned by the new legislation that was part of the reforming temper of the time. The provisions of the

A most significant business

Josias Booker and his brothers established Booker Bros. in Georgetown, West Indies, in 1815. The firm traded in cotton and sugar and later owned plantations in Demerara, one of the three provinces in British Guiana (later Guyana) which had been acquired as a colony by Britain from the Dutch in the late 18th century. The business flourished, and in 1854 the brothers took John McConnell as a partner. Eventually, the Booker family sold out to the McConnells, so that by the end of the 19th century Booker Bros., McConnell & Co. was formed (hereinafter referred to as Booker).

During the 19th century, the company had branched out from trading in produce from the colonial plantations to embrace insurance services, agencies for consumer goods and its own shipping line. It had offices in the heart of the City of London and in Liverpool. It continued to prosper during the early part of the 20th century and it was listed on the London Stock Exchange in 1920. However during the years up to the Second World War, the

low price of sugar, inclement weather and labour issues in British Guiana conspired to dent its profits. All sugar producers began to combine their efforts and Booker merged with an old established firm, Curtis Campbell, in 1939. With this company came J.M. (Jock) Campbell (later Lord Campbell of Eskan), who was

to prove pivotal in the revival of Booker after the Second World War.

Campbell, as managing director from 1952, reorganised and restructured the company, diversifying its activities in British Guiana and the Caribbean, and moving into Africa, Canada and the U.K., encompassing retailing, drug manufacturing, and a printing business. After the colony became independent as Guyana in May 1966 and nationalised its sugar industry,

During the 19th century, the company had branched out to embrace insurance services, agencies for consumer goods and its own shipping line.

Booker's sugar terminal at Demerara.

Booker developed its food distribution and cash-and-carry enterprises, as well as engineering. This latter division included manufacturers of machinery and parts for the sugar industry, pump makers for industrial enterprises, a steel stockholding business, a mining equipment company and a supplier of equipment and systems to the gas and oil industries. The engineering business was the most profitable of Booker's group in the 1970s, but it was eclipsed by the food wholesale and distribution division in the 1990s.

Booker also has a renowned Authors' division. This was formed when Jock Campbell's old friend Ian Fleming, author of the James Bond books, was diagnosed with a terminal illness and asked for advice on how to secure his estate against heavy taxation. Campbell's solution was to acquire a controlling share in the company which handled the royalties from the books and worldwide merchandising (but not film) rights in 1964. Later Booker bought copyrights of other authors, including Agatha Christie's, and the division then contributed significant profits to the firm. The Booker Prize for fiction was launched in 1969.

HSBC Insurance Brokers' connection with Booker came about in 1949, when

Jock Campbell at the Commonwealth Sugar Exporters presentation.

Jock Campbell met his old school friend Michael Robson. At the time, Robson was a director at Antony Gibbs, working at their office at 22 Bishopsgate. Campbell invited Robson to write a report on his group's insurance portfolio; as a result, Robson was asked to join Booker as insurance director.

Michael Robson's son, David, joined Antony Gibbs in 1962 at a time when the work being done for Booker equalled some 50 per cent of the firm's business. David Robson worked on the Booker overseas account and went out to the West Indies, visiting agents on all the

Caribbean islands. Robson recalls that when the World Bank decided to lend money to the world sugar-cane industry for a huge expansion programme, one of the conditions for the loan was that applicants had to employ one of four named consultants as advisors – of which he was one. When the Guyanese government nationalised the insurance industry in the 1980s, Antony Gibbs was appointed its insurance broker.

Antony Gibbs became part of HSBC Insurance Brokers and retained this business until 1993, when the Booker empire began to break up.

Companies Act 1948 and of high taxation were strongly felt by City partnerships such as Antony Gibbs & Sons (which, by this time, had a mixture of family and non-family directors on the board), and like so many firms it chose to become a private limited company.

The post-war expansion of merchant banking activities in North and South America, and in Australia, continued apace, providing at every stage new opportunities for Antony Gibbs & Sons (Insurance) Limited. Under the stimulus of heavy taxation and death duties, and of the need to comply with more stringent employment law, life assurance and pensions business both experienced healthy growth. By 1955, the market for them seemed to justify the formation of a new subsidiary, Antony Gibbs (Life & Pensions) Limited, with offices at 3 Gracechurch Street. Assisted by the parent company's high reputation in many parts of the developing world, the Life and Pensions subsidiary would soon find itself responding to invitations from abroad to establish pensions schemes for a variety of organisations.

Antony Gibbs & Sons (Insurance) Limited, based at 22 Bishopsgate, was by 1960 still a relatively small Lloyd's broker, dealing mainly with the insurance needs of Gibbs connections worldwide. Working life is recalled as "fairly leisurely" in what was effectively a specialist area of a leading merchant bank. The tone emanating from the bank's upper echelons was unashamedly paternalistic, and from the lower ones, deferential. (Members of the Gibbs family who held positions in the firm were addressed by Christian names prefaced by "Mr"; other superiors were "Sir".) A passion for cricket nonetheless united all ranks, from the directors to the lowliest clerk, and the firm mustered an informal team for the Brokers' Cup every year.

In the insurance area, non-marine clients at around this time included the U.K. interests of H.J. Heinz & Co. On the marine side of the business, although there were other large clients such as the container fleet of S. William Coe & Co., the most

A day in the life of a Gibbs broker

David Robson joined Antony Gibbs
(Insurance) Ltd in 1962 and later became
managing director of Gibbs Sage and
Chairman of Gibbs Hartley Cooper before
he resigned in 1985 to manage Anton
Underwriting Agencies, when Lloyd's
required broking firms to divest their Lloyd's
underwriting and member agencies.

Even at 7 o'clock in the morning the heat and
humidity at the private airstrip outside
Georgetown, the capital of Guyana, was sticky.
I was on my way to fly up to visit that country's
largest sugar factory, Albion – the pride of our
clients Booker McConnell. Booker, originally a
British shipping company based in Liverpool,
up to the late 1970s had a finger in every
economic pie in Guyana. It ran seven sugar
factories responsible for producing around
350,000 tons of sugar a year, the shipping fleet
that transported it back to the UK, the sugar
distribution terminal, the largest department
store and much else. No wonder a local, on
hearing an outboard motor on the mighty
Demerara river, commented that even this
motor went "Booker Booker Booker".

The twin-engined (Booker) Cessna rose
quickly into the air and soon the flat coastal
plains were laid out below. I would be asked by
the pilot whether I'd like to enjoy a little "jungle
bashing". This involved flying through the tops
of the trees in the jungle below to put into the
air flocks of the most colourful scarlet ibis. The
green jungle turned literally scarlet beneath us.

After a 40-minute flight the Albion sugar
fields surrounding the factory came into view –
miles of ordered agricultural fields reclaimed
from the surrounding jungle and laid out in
neat blocks divided by irrigation channels.

A car met the plane and it was off to the
general manager's office to go through a
review of the factory's insurance programme,
discuss any claims that might be current, and
hear about the future expansion plans. This
would be followed by a tour of the factory
itself. I never ceased to be amazed at what had
to happen in extracting sugar from a length of
cane. The factory built (of course) by a Booker
company back in Derby was large, noisy, hot
and surrounded by a sticky sweet smell.

A continuous stream of tractors was drawing
up to unload their trailers of what looked like a
jumble of huge matchsticks into the crushing
mills, thus triggering a chain of events which
would result in the white sugar emerging at
the end of the process – something we'd be
taking for granted as we sprinkled it on our
strawberries. Lunch back at the general
manager's house would follow, predominated
by "sugar gossip" from other parts of the
world where I was involved with that industry –
Kenya, Nigeria, Ghana, Jamaica, St Kitts, Peru.

Then back to the airstrip and if time allowed
a detour to climb the Kaieteur Falls. This
involved flying along the gorge straight at the
world's largest drop waterfall (741 ft) and
climbing parallel to the waterfall itself before
levelling out along the river Potari at the top,
an exhilarating experience to say the least.

We would arrive back in Georgetown in time
for the daily relaxing game of tennis. Another
hard day in the life of a Gibbs international
insurance broker in the 1970s was drawing to
a conclusion.

David Robson

important account was still the vast Booker shipping and sugar interest in what was then British Guiana. This was a connection that went back to the 1930s. The Guyanese sugar industry was nationalised in 1970, but Booker's dynamic managing director, Jock Campbell (later Lord Campbell of Eskan), had foreseen this eventuality and directed the company's diversification, both in the U.K. and abroad. Initially the emphasis was on engineering, but the company also built up interests in food wholesaling. By the 1980s Booker was the largest cash-and-carry operator in the U.K., with a highly successful secondary line in health foods and vitamins through its Holland & Barrett retail outlets. Campbell also created the Booker Authors' division, which sponsored the Booker Prize and turned the company name into a household word. The association of Antony Gibbs & Sons (Insurance) Limited with the Booker empire remained close, to the extent that the two companies jointly established Gerrard Insurance Services Ltd in 1986.

The traditional ethos of the City was changing, and pressures to amalgamate

Lionel Sage placed the insurance for De Havilland Aircraft Co.'s Comet Prototype GALVG in March 1950, to provide cover for hull insurance during its demonstration and exhibition period. John Cunningham was named as the principal pilot, but the policy also covered any pilot approved by him. The hull was insured for £350,000 for a period of 12 months. The copy insurance slip was presented to Lionel Sage to commemorate fifty years during which they had provided insurance services to De Havilland.

were beginning to affect all small and medium-sized professional firms. It was decided that the best interests of Antony Gibbs & Sons Ltd. lay in becoming a public limited company, and on going public in 1973 it became Antony Gibbs (Holdings) Ltd. Prompted by the awareness that it must become larger and more comprehensive to survive, Antony Gibbs & Sons (Insurance) Limited began to acquire other small brokers: in 1970, Rose Brothers, established in 1893, which had among its clients the Spangenberg shipping interests and U.K. based May & Baker; in 1973, Chambers McGowan; and in 1974, Andrews Brighton & Holt, formed in 1965. These acquisitions together strengthened the Gibbs insurance presence in specific markets or geographical areas. As a result, the structure of Antony Gibbs & Sons (Insurance) was rationalised in 1974 to create a series of subsidiaries covering all major activities: Marine, International, U.K., Construction, North America, Reinsurance, Pension Services, and Underwriting. There were also subsidiaries for Scotland, and the north-west of England.

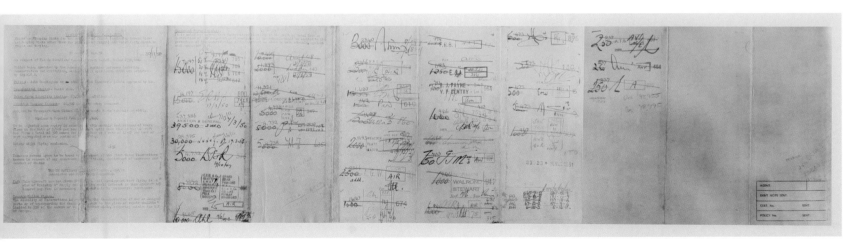

Food for thought

It is always astonishing to find how little the fundamentals of life really alter. According to evidence found by archaeologists, the ancient Greeks and Romans were used to eating porridge, finding, no doubt, that oats are a hardy crop and can be grown even in extremely cold temperatures. Tribes throughout northern Europe used to eat oats too and, when the fashion for them reached Scotland, they were known as "pilcorn". Oatmeal cakes and cheese were part of peasants' diets throughout the Middle Ages, and even in the 17th and 18th centuries, oats gradually replaced barley and rye because they were easier to grow. The Lea family began milling oats in Cheshire in 1675.

As agricultural methods grew more sophisticated, oats took a back seat to wheat but, even so, as long as the principal mode of transport remained the horse, their position in the crop hierarchy was assured. Later, with the Industrial Revolution and the laying of railways, production of oats began to fall and once the motor car took hold, its popularity dived. Until, that is, it became synonymous with healthier living, when it was once again elevated to centre stage.

The oat owed its renaissance to food experts who acknowledged it as a healthy way to start the day. Dr Bircher, a Swiss nutritionist, re-established the old Swiss custom of mixing porridge oats with fresh or dried fruit to create muesli (a German word meaning mixture), a cereal much in favour today. And in more recent years, the well-

Oats were part of Britain's staple diet both during the war and afterwards, when rationing was still in place.

beloved British cook Mrs Beaton began to add oats to her recipes, recommending that they were at their best if taken fresh each day.

The Lea family continued to mill oats steadfastly through more than three and a quarter centuries and their brand, Mornflake, owned by Morning Foods Limited, is still independently owned and managed by the direct descendants of the original millers 14 generations later, with John Lea now at the helm. Instead of milling the oats for farmers, the company now contracts its supply from them, and supplies the milled product to the food industry.

Despite the efforts of the early nutritionists, the popularity of oats was not high during the first half of the 20th century. However, with the start of the

Second World War, Britain's reliance on foodstuffs from beyond its shores clearly had to be rethought, and the demand for home-grown supplies became imperative. Philip Lea, John's father, was in the R.A.F. when he was ordered home to turn crops into food and "feed the nation". The government wanted him to mill oats because it was the healthiest of cereals. There was little scientific knowledge to back this view then, but it is now known that oats contain betan glucan, a soluble fibre that acts like a sponge in absorbing cholesterol and removing it from the body.

The family mills were too small to cope with the task that Philip Lea had been set. The company was able to move to a larger site in Crewe into what was then a derelict flour mill – it had been closed in 1929. Since the country's need was so great, a new mill and factory were built, one of the very few non-munitions developments to take place during the war.

Oats were part of Britain's staple diet both during the war and afterwards, when rationing was still in place. Thereafter, as new and more exciting products became available, Mornflake developed a range of new products which included fruit and nuts as well as oats. Mornflake sells its cereals worldwide, winning the International Grand Medaillon d'Or at the World's Cereal Exhibition as testimony to its success.

Morning Foods was originally a client of Lionel Sage, which has long been merged into HSBC Insurance Brokers. They are responsible for insuring the company's whole business, providing a comprehensive range of covers.

Following this reorganisation, Antony Gibbs & Sons (Insurance) bought Lionel Sage & Co. Ltd in 1976. This medium-sized Lloyd's broker was founded in 1917 by Lionel C. Sage and had a portfolio that was mainly U.K. based, with offices in London and Newport, Wales. It had a strong aviation division, numbering among its clients Hawker Siddeley and De Havilland. It also had some well-known U.K. accounts, including W.R. Royle & Son, the greetings card firm, and Morning Foods, manufacturers of a variety of oat cereal products that had sustained Britain through the war.

With the acquisition of Lionel Sage, Antony Gibbs & Sons (Insurance) – which had already absorbed the other small firms mentioned – almost doubled its broker-age and staff numbers. It also diversified into such areas as aviation and North American surplus lines business. As its then Chairman, Tom Gauge, explained at the time, a small firm must have a variety of specialists in order to serve its clients responsibly, yet the expertise of each might be called upon relatively rarely, making specialists "essential but uneconomical". The merger brought the opportunity to spread existing expertise over a larger portfolio. Moreover, the portfolios of the two companies were complementary, promising a broader-based and more stable busi-ness. Antony Gibbs, Sage Limited, the new company born of the amalgamation, would have premium income in excess of £25 million and be "well-placed to offer a real challenge across the broad range of insurance skills to any of the largest of the quoted brokers".

Hartley Cooper: Lloyd's brokers

TWO BUSINESSES COME TOGETHER

Partnerships, especially in the City of London, have traditionally perpetuated the names of the men who founded them, and the well-remembered Lloyd's broker Hartley Cooper was no exception. There was indeed a Mr James Hartley, just as there was a Mr Edward Ernest Cooper, though a good deal more is known about one than the other.

For most of the 19th century, London was the largest and busiest port in the world. As far upriver as ships could navigate, the Thames was lined with piers and wharves, where vessels from all over the world could tie up, load and unload. Adjacent to the wharves stood warehouses, with ample windows and lifting tackle, to store the goods they brought. Today, many of the names in the redeveloped areas east of the modern London Bridge recall the owners – Hay's Wharf, Butler's Wharf, Chambers' Wharf – and the produce: Cinnamon Buildings, Cotton Wharf, Spice Dock.

James Hartley & Co. is described as "Steam ship brokers and agents" in the fragmentary sources that survive, dated from 1843. James Hartley, his son Bartholomew Hepenstal Hartley, and John Robert Engledue carried on an agency and insurance business and had a warehouse on the south bank of the Thames at Southwark. In 1851 James Hartley was elected to the board of the Marine Insurance Company and thus began a long-lasting connection. The major activity of Hartley's firm was insuring the steamers of the "P&O" – the Peninsular and Oriental Steamship Navigation Company – as they plied the routes between England and various ports in India and

The young E.E. Cooper.

China. A letter from Hartley to the directors of the P&O, dating from May 1858, indicates the importance of the relationship: "our office was established at the instigation of your Board to secure freight to the Company which was being lost to them from the inability of the Local Offices in India and China to meet the requirements of the traffic opened up by your Steamers".

This relationship with the P&O became even closer after 1858, the year in which its original agreement with James Hartley & Co. was extended to remove the need to deal with the local insurers in the Far East. Later, perhaps after the death of his father, Bartholomew Hartley is recorded as having effected all the reinsurances for the London & Oriental Steam Transit Insurance Co., which was taken over by the Marine Insurance Company (of which Engledue was also a director) in about 1876. At that point Engledue left the firm, taking with him the agency side of the business.

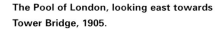

The Pool of London, looking east towards Tower Bridge, 1905.

It is interesting to note that somewhere along the way the firm acquired some "64ths", or shares, in a few steamships – mention of these later appears in the minute books of James Hartley, Cooper & Co., the company created by the merger with E.E. Cooper's firm in 1900.

By then, the sole signatory for the Hartley firm, described in surviving documents as "Shipping agents and Wharfingers", was Arthur Frederick White, one of the two sons (the other being Graham) of Frederick White, a successful Lloyd's broker who was also an underwriter for "the Marine". White (senior) was also connected with the South British Insurance Company, formed by a group of British émigrés to New Zealand, with its headquarters in Auckland and an agency in the City to handle its marine business.

At the time of the merger in 1900, James Hartley & Co. had an office at 19 Leadenhall Street and was one of the dozens of small enterprises clustered around the Royal Exchange, where Lloyd's occupied the first floor, in the heart of the City. No more is known about the Hartleys, father and son, or about their firm, in this period before the merger. In the early 1960s, however, when the Southwark bank of the Thames was being redeveloped, a painted lintel for it was spotted on a derelict wall and photographed by a quick-witted member of the Hartley Cooper staff.

The career of Edward (later Sir Edward) Cooper is better recorded, mainly in the extensive obituary that appeared in *The City Press* on 18 February 1922. He was born in 1848, and joined the Lloyd's broking firm of John Poole in 1867. Two years later he moved to another Lloyd's broker, Henry Head & Co. (An interesting note in Wright and Fayle's *A History of Lloyd's* suggests that Head shared the legendary Cuthbert Heath's interest in widening the insurance offered by Lloyd's, and his concern for financial safeguards.) In 1874, when he was still aged only 27, Edward Cooper's strongly entrepreneurial drive led him to set up on his own. He is said to

The name of James Hartley's firm appears on the lintel of this Southwark warehouse, which was demolished during the area's redevelopment in the 1970s.

have treasured his original ticket of membership of Lloyd's, where he carried on business as both broker and underwriter for the next 30 years, though the latter activity was personal and kept completely separate from the brokerage.

As a young Lloyd's broker, Edward Cooper would probably have been working exclusively in the field of marine insurance. To assist him with what was clearly a thriving business, Cooper employed his brother Charles. Colonel Sidney (later Sir Sidney) Wishart joined them in 1887, and Charles Bland in 1888. An agreement commencing on 1 January 1894 identifies the point at which Edward Cooper, Charles Cooper and Sidney Wishart became partners in a firm to be styled E.E. Cooper & Co., with offices at 4 Bishopsgate. The arrangement was highly favourable to Edward Cooper, who put up £2000 of the £3000 founding capital and was to receive two-thirds of any profits. While the other two men were obliged to devote their entire energies to the business, Edward Cooper was left free to pursue other interests and to have unlimited clerical support from the partnership in doing so.

It was as this agreement was reaching the end of its seven-year term that the merger took place that created the new firm of James Hartley, Cooper & Co. The three partners of Cooper's firm and Arthur White of James Hartley & Co. almost certainly came to know one another through the transaction of marine insurance. However it came about, the respective parties must have believed that the businesses complemented each other. An agreement taking effect from 31 December 1900 sets out how E.E. Cooper & Co. and James Hartley & Co. were each to be wound up, and their premises and their goodwills bought by the newly created James Hartley, Cooper & Co. for £54,000 and £21,000 respectively. Of 7500 Preference shares created, Edward Cooper was allocated 3500 and the other signatories lesser numbers, but all except Charles Cooper were bound to subscribe for Ordinary shares in cash (although no share value is mentioned): Cooper and Wishart for 2000 each

The entrepreneurial E.E. Cooper.

and White for 1950. The three men were obliged to retain at least half of these shares while they remained directors. This tidy arrangement gave the newly formed brokerage some running capital with which to begin life.

Two highly significant events resulted from the triangular relationship of White (senior) with the Hartley firm, "the Marine" and "the South British". The first was that, as manager and underwriter of the Marine, White had appointed as its New York agent a gentleman called Percy Chubb, heir to an insurance concern called Chubb & Son that began in 1882. Although still small at the time, the Chubb connection passed to James Hartley, Cooper & Co., eventually giving rise to what would prove to be the firm's most important client relationship of the next 70 years. The second came when – although the exact date is unknown – James Hartley, Cooper &

The Lloyd's underwriting room, on the first floor of the Royal Exchange pre-1928.

Facing Page:
The partnership agreement, dated 27 December 1900, between the partners of E.E. Cooper & Co. and Arthur White of James Hartley & Co. to create the new company James Hartley, Cooper & Co.

Filed 27th December 1900

This Agreement made the 27th day of December 1900 Between Edward Ernest Cooper Sidney Wishart and John Charles Cooper all of 4 Bishopsgate Street in the City of London Insurance Brokers of the first part Arthur Frederick White of 19 Leadenhall Street in the City of London Insurance Broker of the second part and James Hartley Cooper & Company Limited whose registered office is at 4 Bishopsgate Street aforesaid (hereinafter called "the Company") of the third part Whereas the said Edward Ernest Cooper Sidney Wishart

Co. took offices in a tall, thin building called Jerusalem Chambers, Cowper's Court. It was just off Cornhill and only steps from Lloyd's, in a corner of the City that retains the atmosphere of a bygone era even today. Resident at Jerusalem Chambers since 1881 was one Septimus Merriman, the London agent of the South British Insurance Company. In 1904, the South British bought the building. From then until 1935, when it moved to other offices in Lime Street, it would be both landlord and close associate of James Hartley, Cooper & Co. In time, it would take a small financial interest in the firm, and perhaps by its move in 1935 it occasioned the firm's own move to 85 Gracechurch Street.

Building Prosperity

Edward Cooper was the nominal head of James Hartley, Cooper & Co., but his other interests meant that increasingly it was Col. Sidney Wishart who was its acting head and Charles Bland who as secretary oversaw its day-to-day running. From 1902 Wishart led the firm's marine underwriting syndicate at Lloyd's. (From 1916, it would have two. The other known by the name of F.R. Bussell, the first underwriter, dealt mainly with non-marine business and was later led by George Deverell, who joined the firm as an office boy but showed such remarkable talent that he ended up on the board!)

Edward Cooper is reported to have been a genial man, full of bonhomie, with a deep love of music and a splendid singing voice. He sang in London choirs, notably that of St Paul's Cathedral, all his life; he was a patron of St Paul's Choir School, a liveryman of the Musicians' Company from 1905 and, later, its Master. (William Crocker in *Tales from the Coffee House* (1973) recalled Cooper's encouragement of

Colonel Sidney Wishart (right), with H.W. Bunton (left) at Jerusalem Chambers.

LLOYD'S GOLF CLUB

IMPORTANT

The Committee wish to draw the attention of all Members to the rules regarding the marking of competition cards.

Recently at Lloyd's meetings there has been a marked increase in the number of cards returned which have not complied with the rules.

In future any competitor submitting a card incorrectly marked will be disqualified

F. M. CARLISLE,

M. ILLINGWORTH,

Hon. Secretaries

Edward Cooper was the first of five presidents of the Lloyd's Golf Club with an HSBC connection. Miles Illingworth was a director of Antony Gibbs and Sons (Insurance) for many years.

a promising young organist and singer, for whom he found a job at James Hartley, Cooper & Co.: that is, until extracurricular musical activities came to take up what Cooper considered a disproportionate amount of the young man's time, and he was advised to rethink his priorities.) In 1909 Cooper became an Alderman of Cornhill Ward and later, Sheriff. Also in 1909, he became President of the Lloyd's Golf Club, with which he already had a long association. He was knighted in 1913. Once Col. Wishart too became involved in civic affairs, Charles Bland took a more prominent role, being made a director in 1914.

By this time there were many established businesses in Lloyd's, some of which were both brokers and underwriters. These firms included: Bland Welch & Co., C.T. Bowring, Glanvill Enthoven, Dumas & Wylie, Alexander Howden, Rose Brothers, H.B. Sedgwick & Co. and Willis Faber & Co. Figures drawn from the minute books of James Hartley, Cooper & Co. Ltd suggest that from the start it justified the founders' confidence. Even in its first year, earnings showed a surplus over expenditure, to yield pre-tax profits of nearly £23,000. This amount was divided among the shareholders – these being Cooper, Wishart, Arthur and Graham White, and one or two family members to whom they had sold or given shares. For the next 20 years earnings would continue on a strong upward curve, and while the growing firm's expenses naturally increased over the same period, they did so much less rapidly. The years of the greatest increases in earnings were those of the Great War, 1914 to 1918. By 1920, with earnings of £253,000 and expenses of £48,000, pre-tax profits stood at an astonishing £205,000.

The share structure made the entry into the firm of the sons of the directors almost automatic, assuming that they had an aptitude for the work. In 1910 new shares to the value of £100,000 were created (bringing the company's total share capital to £250,000), and the directors were left free to "hold, sell, allot or otherwise dispose of" the new shares as they saw fit. Some of these shares would be offered to senior employees in the years to come, but the number of shareholders always remained small and many were related in some way to the original directors. Some have described the atmosphere of the office as "like a family", perhaps because, to some degree, it *was* a family, yet there was apparently no favouritism towards the next generation of directors: only the certainty that much would be expected of them.

What kind of insurance broking did the firm undertake in its formative first two decades? Initially almost all of it would have been marine related, for clients such as the Bristol Steam Navigation Company (still a client 60 years later), but by 1920 the biggest earner was Fire insurance. Employers' Liability was well established, while Motor and Aviation were growth areas. But a new opportunity from across the Atlantic had presented itself in the early years of the century. In addition to the connection with Chubb & Son that has already been mentioned, James Hartley, Cooper & Co. acquired a number of large American banks as clients.

The origin of this bank insurance business reveals the adaptability that had made Lloyd's great. The early 20th century was an era in which the highly diversified U.S. banking system was suffering greatly from the activities of criminals. Much of this was simple burglary or "night robbery" (as opposed to the armed raid, or "daylight" robbery) which could be insured against through a Burglary policy tailored to an individual location. But much theft and fraud was perpetrated by banks' own employees: inside informants, clerks with hands in the till, forgers and the like. Against such persons the only protection was the individual fidelity bond, which for multiple employees was clearly expensive and unwieldy. In the face of so much employee-related crime, the banks were eager to obtain more comprehensive insurance, while for their part the native U.S. insurers were understandably reluctant to provide it.

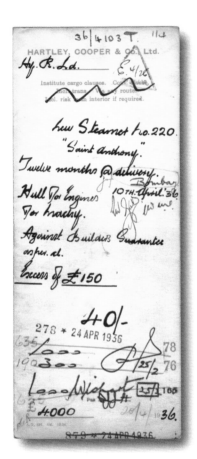

This slip was handwritten by Percy Whales, cargo director. Each slip would normally have the prefix V or H (Voyage or Hull), which enabled the Accounts department to credit brokerage to the correct department.

As former Lloyd's underwriter John Twitchett put it in 1991, in his study of the early links between Lloyd's and the American banks, "the requirements of the US banking industry anxious to find cover to protect themselves against the losses incurred during the process of their business" presented a challenge. Lloyd's rose to it by devising the "bankers' blanket bond" policy. As its name suggests, this was an insurance policy that covered a bank's risk from its employees on a "blanket" basis – in other words, as a group, and individually within the group. Although the earliest instance of similar cover seems to have dated from 1907, the whole subject comes onto firmer ground with the passing of the Lloyd's Act of 1911. John Twitchett claims that the first true bankers' blanket bond policy was issued in June of that year by James Hartley, Cooper & Co. in favour of the First National Bank of Boston, and that the risk was shared among a number of leading Lloyd's syndicates.

The document reputed to be the first bankers' blanket bond policy, dated 4th May 1911, now in the possession of HSBC Insurance Brokers.

While the American insurers protested that such cover was irresponsible, they were at last prompted to compete with Lloyd's by developing their own. Nonetheless, the reputation of Lloyd's was irresistible and the amount of North American bank insurance placed in London advanced steadily. James Hartley, Cooper & Co. was in the vanguard of this business from the start, thanks to close collaboration with Hubert Augustus Nicholls, the underwriter who devised the Lloyd's Bankers' Policy forms, revised many times over the years and colloquially known as HAN forms. The firm's greatest asset, however, was Russell Fawcus, a director of the firm from 1918, who had excellent personal contacts among the banks in North America, particularly with J.F. Hayden & Co. of Montreal, which handled a great deal of American bank insurance.

The war years, 1914 to 1918, saw the majority of the firm's men in the armed forces, while a skeleton staff managed affairs at Jerusalem Chambers. A company Roll of Honour records that of the 59 employees and 3 directors who enlisted, 13 were killed. One – Walter Cooper, the nephew of Edward Cooper – was awarded the Military Cross. To those who returned to Cowper's Court with the coming of peace, the years before 1914 seemed like a lost age of innocence. An immediate post-war boom was followed by rampant inflation. Those returning from war service received a payment of half-salary dating from their enlistment. Times were harder for those who had held the fort in London. Three surviving letters to the directors from such men respectfully beg the payment of War Bonus or other financial recognition of sacrifices made. What immediate response they received is unknown. In 1920, however, came a major restructuring of the company, with the liquidation of James Hartley, Cooper & Co., its re-formation as Hartley Cooper & Co., an increase in share capital, and provision for a wider distribution of shares.

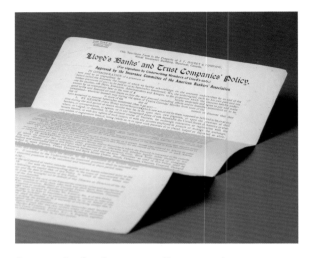

An example of an insurance policy arranged with J.F. Hayden & Co. of Montreal.

Between the Wars

Hartley Cooper was now a well-established and respected Lloyd's broker. Its reputation was enhanced by the election of Sir Edward Cooper as Lord Mayor of London for the mayoral year 1919–20. In that same year Col. Wishart served as Sheriff, and in 1921 he too was knighted, becoming Col. Sir Sidney Wishart. Sadly, Sir Edward Cooper died in 1922. He was succeeded as Chairman by Wishart, the originator of the Bankers Guarantee Policy (colloquially known as the "Hartley Cooper A form") that remained in use until the 1930s.

Despite the war and its aftermath, working conditions in the City had altered little since the early years of the century. Most employees commuted some distance to work, usually by rail or underground, but often, by bicycle or on foot. The working week included Saturday mornings, and would continue to do so until well into the 1950s. In an era of such economic instability and high unemployment, deference reigned, and in this Jerusalem Chambers was no different from any other office. Colleagues were addressed as "Mr" and telephone use was restricted to two directors. The usual mode of overseas communication was by cable, followed by letter; correspondence was acknowledged on the day it was received, and written with steel pens. Professional status and seniority were apparent from the way a man dressed. As contemporary photographs show, suits, white shirts and ties were standard attire for everyone, but hats were indicators of rank, especially in the City, with top hats the prerogative of company chairmen, bowlers reserved for directors or partners, and the softer varieties for the lower orders. Brokers, who were out and about for a good part of the day, are recalled as having worn trilbys or other brimmed hats. The detachable collar, early on made of celluloid but by the 1920s of heavily starched cotton, was part of the unofficial City uniform and would remain so into the 1960s.

Sir Edward Ernest Cooper, painted in robes and regalia, as Lord Mayor of the City of London, 1919–20.

The sport of kings

Hartley Cooper's Bloodstock division, which has arranged insurance for all types of livestock since the 1920s, acquired a considerable reputation, especially with the horse-racing fraternity.

The division's main source of business was the Kentucky Insurance Agency Inc. which was owned by a roll call of entrepreneurs famous for their horse breeding and stud farms in Kentucky, U.S.A. Leslie Combs II, for example, bought Spendthrift Farm in 1937 and named it after the horse that ran as a youngster in 1878 for his great-grandfather, Daniel Swigert, who built up a high profile enterprise breeding yearlings that went on to win major races. Warren Wright, another owner in the agency, had taken over Calumet Farm from his father William Monroe Wright in 1932

Pictured from left to right: Roger and Beth Bassett, Sandy and John Jewiss (Managing Director of Hartley Cooper), Lester Piggott (jockey), and Geoffrey Summers (Secretary of JAGB).

and developed it into a very successful thoroughbred farm, breeding and training many well-known winners. In time, the Kentucky Insurance Agency became the largest bloodstock insurance agency in the world and it continued to provide Hartley Cooper with a great deal of business right through to the 1960s, when it broke up. Other agencies which had appointed Hartley Cooper as brokers included Blair Scott & Co., Dominion Co., also based in Kentucky, and Centaur Insurance Brokers. Hartley Cooper subsequently purchased

this agency and renamed its Bloodstock division after it, so that it traded as Centaur for some time.

The Bloodstock division was also well respected in the British racing industry and took an active part in sponsoring races. Sponsorship included offering a special award of a diamond in a casket to any jockey who won six races in a row during the 1983 and 1984 flat racing seasons, and sponsoring races at high profile courses such as Doncaster and Redcar and even the Jersey Derby in 1984.

The Bloodstock division was also well respected in the British racing industry and took an active part in sponsoring races.

Derby Day at Epsom Downs was particularly exciting in 1984 because the insurance for the winner, Secreto, previously arranged by Hartley Cooper for a specific amount, suddenly needed to be increased in line with the horse's new, more valuable status.

Hartley Cooper was appointed as broker for the Jockeys' Association of Great Britain (JAGB) and arranged cover which included a weekly benefit scheme for leading jockeys. The firm was also appointed broker for Racing Management Services, arranging some rather out of the ordinary cover, such as insurance for the Vladivar Vodka Company, which offered a £150,000 prize if a horse managed to break the world record for a five-furlong sprint at Epsom. It was through an introduction from JAGB that Hartley Cooper participated in presentations for new business at jockey clubs in Hong Kong and Singapore.

Hartley Cooper was also indirectly involved in the insurance of the famous racehorse Shergar, whose disappearance in 1983 caused such a stir. Shergar was originally owned solely by H.H. the Aga Khan, but after the horse's spectacular wins he decided to maximise his investment by selling shares to a

Secreto beating El Gran Senor at Epsom on Derby Day 1984.

syndicate. One of the purchasers of a share was Sir Philip Oppenheimer, who owned his own considerable bloodstock interests in the U.K., for which Hartley Cooper arranged insurance. Sir Philip was one of the few members of the syndicate whose own brokers arranged insurance

for a share of Shergar and, since his cover included theft, he was paid in full when the horse was kidnapped.

Hartley Cooper was purchased by HSBC in September 1983 and its Bloodstock division, with its long-standing reputation as experts in the field, continued as a small but significant division of HSBC Insurance Brokers for a few more years.

One of the most memorable events of the interwar period was Lloyd's departure from the Royal Exchange, where since 1844 it had occupied the first floor. For the first time since its coffee-house days Lloyd's had a home of its own, a handsome and spacious building in Lime Street that opened in 1928. At its heart was "the Room", with its underwriters' boxes, numbered and arranged in syndicates, and a central covered rostrum accommodating the Caller and the Lutine Bell displayed above him.

Cowper's Court at about the same time is recalled as having a Dickensian air, with much mahogany panelling and open fires in winter. Of the firm's various departments, the most important was the American department, with its marine and non-marine sections, boasting a clutch of major financial institutions as clients. Foremost among these was the Chubb insurance empire, which had grown along with the century. By this time it had offices and depots all over the world and placed a large amount of reinsurance in the London market via Hartley Cooper. Now heading the company was Hendon Chubb, younger brother of Percy; like him, he was an Anglophile whom many at Hartley Cooper came to know personally. Chubb, together with the banking clients such as Bank of America, First National City Bank of New York, First National Bank of Boston, Crocker Bank and Wells Fargo, were looked after personally by Russell Fawcus and were Hartley Cooper's most important clients between the wars. The Bank of Bermuda's long association with Hartley Cooper also dates from the 1920s.

The Home department had marine and non-marine sections, but there was also the Marine department (divided into "Hull" and "Cargo"), impressively international, with clients and connections in The Netherlands, Belgium and Germany, and farther afield in India and the Far East. Important risks for which insurance was broked in the late 1920s included the many cargoes of steel for the construction of the Sydney Harbour Bridge, and prominent among the "Hull" clients was Japan's

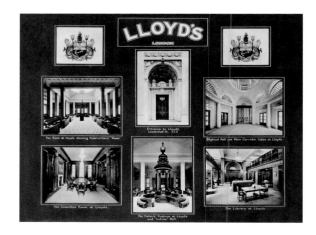

A montage of photographs of Lloyd's new building, which opened in 1928.

A day in the life of an office boy in the early 1920s

I joined the firm of James Hartley, Cooper & Co. Ltd in June 1920, as office boy in the Policy department.

In those days the firm's offices were at 2 Cowper's Court, in an early Victorian building known as Jerusalem Chambers. The Policy department was situated at the top of the main two-storey building and was reached by ascending a rickety wooden staircase. The heating of the department was supplied by a large coal-burning open fireplace so that the person sitting with his or her back to the fire got more than his or her share of the fire. Others weren't quite so lucky as there was a constant stream of people going to and from the French department situated on the third floor of the General Accident building in Birchin Lane. At the top of this building the typists (three or four) had an office dominated by Miss Hogg. The electric lighting was very primitive, the flex being frayed in various places, and the switches were of the old-fashioned brass type. I am still amazed that I never knew of anyone being electrocuted – they were constantly short-circuiting.

This brings me to my job. I would arrive at about 9.15 am (London, Brighton & South Coast Railway permitting) and get out of a safe boxes which contained policies awaiting completion. I then had to mark up the registers – two loose-leafed ledgers (one for 'time'

policies and the other for 'voyage' policies) which contained a record of each policy and its present whereabouts. My next job was to collect policies for Inland Revenue stamping. This consisted of listing the policies and their respective due stamps, totalling the stamps and taking them over to the Inland Revenue Stamp Office which was then in Austin Friars. One was allowed 15 specials at any one time, the remainder were left for subsequent collection in the afternoon or next day. Woe betide you if you tried to slip in more than 15 specials at any one time. On returning from the Stamp Office in the morning I would have to file policies which were copied in a loose-leafed ledger and index them. The only policies which were copied were the non-marine policies prepared on the only typewriter and a few non-marine and hull policies which were hand-written in copying ink (these were copied with the aid of a huge press which stood just inside the entrance to the Policy department). This process required great skill! Any time left in the morning I would turn to writing marine policies (these were not copies).

Lunch-time was a bit elastic although it was officially from 1 pm to 2 pm. On returning to the office in the afternoon I would go through the same procedure for stamping as in the morning. All my work was punctuated by journeys to the Accounts department situated

at 29 Cornhill, above the Scottish Widows offices, with special policies to be journalised.

On return from the Stamp Office it was my job to fill the kettle for afternoon tea (made by one of the ladies). The water was boiled over the open fire in winter or on a dilapidated electric stove in summer. Having filled the kettle it was my job to go round to each member of the Policy department and take his or her order for cakes etc. These were mostly obtained from Messrs Lyons & Co. in Gracechurch Street at the corner of Leadenhall Market entrance (this aspect of my job was rather demeaning!). The remainder of the afternoon was spent writing policies to send to the Accounts department, with more often than not a further visit to Accounts with a "must be posted tonight" special policy – in this respect I was very unpopular with Accounts! To finish my day's work I would have to return the boxes of policies awaiting completion to the safe in a small room adjacent to the Policy department and would then "slink away" (perhaps a little before 6 pm) home. I thought myself lucky if I did not encounter Mr Atwell on the stairs!

I worked in the Marine Policy department for about two years and wasn't sorry to become attached to the non-marine side of policy preparing where there were a few more typewriters.

My successor as office boy was John Trendall who made various alterations in the duties, e.g. not being available when it was time to fill the kettle and go for cakes!

Fred Nicholl

Sumitomo Marine & Fire Insurance Company. Among the U.K. non-marine clients was the U.K.'s largest wholesale tobacco distributor, Palmer & Harvey, with its fleet of vans.

The Dickensian tone of Hartley Cooper's offices was not to last much longer, for by 1934 there was simply no more room in Cowper's Court or in the two Birchin Lane buildings the firm now occupied. Perhaps the sale of Jerusalem Chambers was the last straw, but another factor was almost certainly the desire to be closer to the Lloyd's building in Lime Street. Purpose-built office accommodation was being erected all over the City, and after calculating that it needed some 7500 square feet of space, Hartley Cooper took the third floor of 85 Gracechurch Street – described at the time as "the last word in planning, convenience and administration". In time Hartley Cooper also came to occupy half of the second and half of the fourth floors.

While Hartley Cooper was undoubtedly a paternalistic firm, it was also highly professional. Departments were efficiently run: their various heads were "excellent administrators: unflappable, longserving, experienced problem-solvers", and the atmosphere of the office is recalled as being "civilised". Daily, as brokers arrived at the office, the department heads would allocate to them the renewal business that appeared in the departmental diary, or items of new business that had to be researched. All business and terms were "translated" onto the brokers' slips with meticulous accuracy. The importance of this, as staff were told constantly, could not be overestimated, since the relationship between Lloyd's brokers and Lloyd's underwriters depended on absolute trust. (The comment of one department head on this point – "five years to build a reputation and five seconds to lose it!" – entered the lore of the firm and was still being repeated 30 years later.)

With the wording on his slips agreed with his department head, the broker could set off for Lloyd's. The individual broker's existence could appear unstructured to

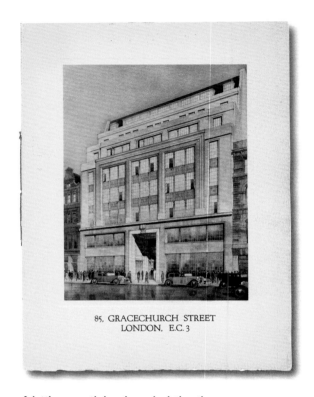

85, GRACECHURCH STREET
LONDON. E.C. 3

A letting agent's brochure depicting the new offices at 85 Gracechurch Street, into which Hartley Cooper moved in 1935. Directly opposite was the London office of the Hongkong and Shanghai Banking Corporation.

Facing Page:
City workers in front of the Lloyd's building, marching purposefully to their offices in the early 1950s.

outsiders, but in reality was anything but. (As one veteran recalls, "If you were going to speak to 50 or 60 people in the course of a day, you had to get a move on.") Regular conversations with other brokers and underwriters over coffee were partly social occasions and partly business: they not only produced useful information about what was going on in a particular market, but helped a broker – especially a young one – to become a good judge of character and, metaphorically speaking, to "read between the lines".

Once the Room was open, the broker made the rounds of the underwriters, seated with their deputies and clerks at the famous "boxes", which were rather like long school desks equipped with bookshelves and benches. Syndicates with an interest in a similar class of business sat near one another, and the experienced broker usually knew which underwriter to approach for a quotation, depending on the risks he had to place.

In presenting a risk, the broker produced his slip, a large sheet of grey or cream card folded accordion-style, bearing the administrative details of his firm on the section farthest to the left. The adjacent portion of the form contained the information about the client and the cover being sought: this was the "who, what, when, why, where?" section, over which such pains had to be taken to ensure completeness and clarity. The remaining sections were for the underwriters to fill in with the figures showing the percentage of the risk each was prepared to take, the date, and his initials. A special stamp next to all this showed the syndicate to which the underwriter belonged. The "lead" underwriter would be the first to respond to the broker's combination of practical knowledge and market savvy by accepting a proportion of the risk – say, 10 per cent, and writing this, with his name and other details, on the slip. With his confidence reinforced, the broker then made his way around the Room until he had managed to place the whole of his risk. Only then could he head back to his

The offices of James Hartley, Cooper & Co. at Jerusalem Chambers, Cowper's Court where they remained from 1904 until 1935. Above, from left to right, Graham White, Charles Bland and Herbert Garrett.

Recollections of Cowper's Court

Written by John Francis (Hartley Cooper, 1926–72) in 1981 in response to a letter in the house magazine claiming that there had been rats at Jerusalem Chambers.

Regarding No. 2 Cowper's Court, I think one floor, the third, top one, had certain Dickensian overtones. Mr Bishop (of Calcutta sweepstake fame) held a sort of sway with Harry Band and John Trendall in support. It was the Policy office, usually ankle-deep in paper (rather like the present underwriting room at closing time if one may apply that term). It looked out over the "slates" of EC3 with their smoking chimney stacks and cast-iron gutters. It was a hive of industry where the term "Raving urgent" was coined. There were no rats up there, as some have suggested – only the ladies' room. Whether that was up to the standard of *Oliver Twist* I cannot vouch for.

Coming down a floor was a large open-plan office with windows over Cowper's Court presided over by Mr Doublet (Returns) and Mr Freddie Wood (Cover). Everyone was Mr in those days and it wouldn't enter my head even now to refer to them as Doublet and Wood. Mr D. was a formidable character who when suffering acutely from his almost universal and painful condition needed careful handling.

Below that was the General Office resplendent with dark mahogany woodwork, approached through swing doors to a mahogany "barrier".

A handsome office with the Advising department (presided over by Mr Frank Miskin), two rows of us, included Bill Rankin, myself and two ladies who checked our debit notes. These were handwritten with steel pens and printing ink. In the corner near the barrier stood the iron press on which debits were printed after damping. There was a fireplace where there was a splendid coal fire in winter. Steps led down to Mr Lindley's Room. Along one side of the General Office were a series of small offices for directors, shielded discreetly by frosted glass in mahogany frames, in which sat Mr Hough, Mr Garrett, Colonel Cooper, Mr Fawcus and Mr Bland at the end. Outside Mr Fawcus's door sat Mr Callow (American department). There was a bell which buzzed to summon him to the presence when his boss needed him.

At the end of the room was Marine with Messrs Ransome, Whale, Gold, Winter and others, and beyond them a door which led through to the Birchin Lane office where such lesser lights as Non-marine and Accounts plied their trade. Birchin Lane and the Glasshouse are a separate story.

I haven't yet mentioned the Chairman, Col. Sir Sidney Wishart, whose office lay just up the stairs from the main entrance in Cowper's Court. He was an almost God-like figure, seldom seen, of whom it was rumoured by us small fry that even the directors stood in awe. He was attended by Bill Pillow, last survivor of a dying race, the male typist. He was a rather flustered greying little chap who was said to have courted Mrs Pillow for 16 years before popping the question.

Great characters each and every one, and there was Chris Johnson, the craftiest broker of all, who died on the steps of the Royal Exchange. It was said (probably apocryphally) that on hearing the news the Chairman said, "Where is his slip case?" to Freddie Gough, the broker who would be dropped at Arnhem, an M.C. and subsequently M.P.

There was Arthur Garrett in spats, a tremendous non-marine broker in a small frail frame who taught many of us our trade…

…and a string of charming ladies – like great actresses they retained their maiden names whether married or not; that was the convention.

It was most definitely a happy ship. We had many a laugh, not least when an excitable young broker emptied the out-tray over someone who could be sharp at times. The old place was, I think, called Jerusalem Chambers and the South British had the floor below. Thus was laid the great development of the firm we now know. Sir Edward Cooper (whose bronze plaque still hangs in Cornhill on the wall of the Union Discount), Col. Sir Sidney Wishart and those who came after them laid soundly. To them I partly owe the pension I draw, and to all those good-looking, smart and present-day members I can only say that there were certainly no rats about. Perhaps there is some confusion with what I believe is now called the rat-race.

John Francis

office with a feeling of satisfaction. Once there, he would contact his clients, report to his department head, and address the paperwork needed to confirm and record each transaction.

The brokers' efforts were of course backed up by teams of clerk-typists at Jerusalem Chambers. The work of the Policy office required particular attention. The majority of policies were produced on pre-printed forms (the HAN form in its successively revised versions) and onto these the typists had to transfer the information from the slips that had been broked at Lloyd's. Some policies, especially those for the American banks, had to be prepared using handmade paper, and if a

Bateman cartoon:
Dynamic effect of a black cat entering the room at Lloyd's, or 'Welcome'.

The underwriting room at Lloyd's between the wars.

mistake was made, the whole policy had to be retyped. These handmade policies had to be verified with the lead underwriter whose terms appeared on the slip, and usually this entailed a trip to the Room. The hive of activity there never failed to impress the young clerks, and brought home to them just how far-reaching was the business of which they were a part.

For all the formality, custom and tradition that dictated procedures at Lloyd's, there was a fair amount of humour in the daily round. The Room was known for its practical jokes and the outlandishness of some of the risks placed there (the risks of capturing the Loch Ness Monster, or of long beards catching fire, come to mind). Jasper Gold, Hartley Cooper's head cargo broker and a source of memorable jokes, managed to place a line of insurance at Christmas one year by distracting the underwriter. It was for "elephants in paper bags and steam in crates". (This surely ranks alongside the story told by William Crocker in *Tales from the Coffee House* about the newcomer to the Room who was sent to get a copy of the "quill and gimlet exclusion" from the revered Hubert Nicholls.) Lloyd's before the war was "an extraordinarily nice place to be in and out of"; there were always congenial and interesting people, a good deal of wit, and the sense that one was involved with every aspect of life, "from twins to crematoria".

The 1930s were of course coloured by the Great Depression that followed the Wall Street Crash of 1929, and by the ominous political events abroad that led inexorably to war in 1939. In the United States there arose a degree of resentment against Lloyd's among the American insurers of financial institutions. A delegation from London, in which Hartley Cooper was represented by Russell Fawcus, succeeded in allaying the mistrust and reaching an "Agreement with Surety Companies" and a "Reinsurance Agreement" in 1935.

Administratively this was an unsettled period for Hartley Cooper: there was the

Russell Fawcus, a director of James Hartley, Cooper & Co., whose excellent contacts with American banks brought the firm so much business. Business was also obtained through Adams & Porter, Betts Brothers and Cornwell & Stevens.

H.M.S. *Belfast*

H.M.S. *Belfast* was the last in a long line of big gun ships built specifically to protect the trade routes which were part of Britain's empire. The vessel was built by Harland & Wolff in Belfast as an 11,553 ton cruiser, with an overall length of 187 metres and a maximum speed of 32 knots. She was launched on 17 March 1938 and she was commissioned into the Royal Navy on 5 August 1939, just in time for the commencement of the Second World War. At the peak of her service, she was home to 950 officers and men whose living conditions, cramped and overcrowded as they were, would have raised a few eyebrows today.

Although the early months of the war are often referred to as the "phoney war" in Britain, the navy was engaged in action from the start. At the outbreak of war, H.M.S. *Belfast* formed part of the 18th Cruiser Squadron based in Scapa Flow in the Orkney Islands. She was successful at intercepting enemy ships very early on, but on 21 November 1939 she was blown up by a mine as she was leaving the Firth of Forth. The damage

was considerable and repairs took over two years; she did not return to duty until 3 November 1942, when she rejoined the fleet as the flagship of the 10th Cruiser Squadron.

As part of the squadron, her role was to provide cover for the merchant ships which were trying to keep the supply routes open. In 1943, the orders were to protect convoys of ships delivering supplies to and returning from Russian ports. At one point the fleets of the navy's Force 1 and Force 2 were required to provide cover for three

convoys heading east to deliver their cargo, and two heading west on their return journey. H.M.S. *Belfast* was part of Force 1 and saw considerable action, with the fleet of Force 2 succeeding in sinking the *Scharnhorst* on 21 December 1943, and as part of the strike force which sank the *Tirpitz* in 1944.

The ship played its part in Operation Neptune, the naval operations which supported the D-Day landings on 6 June 1944, the purpose of which was to clear the way on the beaches of Normandy for troops to land. She was the first cruiser

to begin the bombardment for the invasion.

After the war H.M.S. *Belfast* took up her role of protecting the citizens of the British Empire in the Far East. She ferried British prisoners of war who had been released from Japanese camps in Shanghai and Hong Kong to safety, and she remained as part of the peace-keeping force until she returned to Portsmouth on 15 October 1947. She was recommissioned just under a year later for further service in the Far East, as countries in the region fought for their independence. She was also active during two years of the Korean War as part of the British and Commonwealth fleet, bombarding the shore to provide protection to troops after North Korea crossed the 38th Parallel in July 1950. She then returned to Britain to be refitted and modernised, and her final tour of duty for the navy in the years from 1959 to 1963 was in her traditional role of protecting British interests.

H.M.S. *Belfast* was finally paid off on 24 August 1963 and retired from active service in 1965. The decision was taken for her to be preserved as an example of her kind (the first Royal Navy ship to be preserved for the British nation

since Nelson's H.M.S. *Victory*) and, after some refitting and preparation, she was bought to London and opened to the public on 21 October 1971. Now owned by the Imperial War Museum and commanding an excellent position on the south side of the river Thames, with the Tower of London and Tower Bridge

as her backdrop, H.M.S. *Belfast* was insured at Lloyd's during its construction by Hartley Cooper. The original Lloyd's slip is displayed on board the ship. She is distinguished as the only surviving example of the big guns armoured warships which Britain built for its navy during the first half of the 20th century.

The ship played its part in Operation Neptune, the naval operations which supported the D-Day landings in 1944.

move to Gracechurch Street, there was the death of Col. Sir Sidney Wishart and the retirement in 1938 of Charles Bland, who had succeeded Wishart as Chairman. (Reginald Lindley, who succeeded Bland, himself died in 1940 and was succeeded by Fawcus, who was to hold office until 1953.) Over all, there loomed the uncertainty of the international situation. No figures survive to indicate how this prevailing uncertainty might have been translated into a heightened requirement for insurance.

Similarly, there are few documents to suggest how the firm fared during six years of war, with all the dangers that a location in the heart of the bombarded City implied. A handwritten note from 1938 records the formation of an Air Raid Protection unit

Hartley Cooper's Accounts department at 85 Gracechurch Street in the late 1930s. An excellent example of a clear desk policy.

The day war broke out

The day war broke out was a Sunday, so Hartley Cooper's emergency plans did not come into operation until Monday 4 September. I was employed in the Non-Marine Policy department (the forerunner of today's non-marine services), and in common with the rest of the staff at 85 Gracechurch Street, except for brokers and a minimum of back-up of typists and clerks, I had orders to report to Summerfield House, Elstree. This was a Victorian mansion which the firm had acquired as evacuation headquarters. It stood in four acres of well-kept grounds in the centre of the village.

As I was a south Londoner this was strange country to me, but I duly made my way by tube to Golders Green, where I witnessed the never-to-be-forgotten sight of hundreds of young school children being taken by tube and bus to dispersal points ready for evacuation – bewildered, frightened and yet often excited kids, each with his bag or bundle of clothes, and his gas mask in a cardboard box slung over his shoulder. Arriving after a long delay at Edgware I found my colleagues and the staff of Bowrings queuing for the infrequent bus service to Elstree and Borehamwood, where Bowrings had taken over the film studios as offices. Rising magnificently to the occasion, the bus inspector diverted every bus arriving at Edgware that morning to Elstree.

Incredible as it may seem, some work was done that day as an advance party had brought office furniture and files from the City the previous week, and in a few days we were in full production again. Summerfield House became our home from Monday to Friday for the next six months, when all but the Accounts department returned to the City. This was as a matter of fact just before the air raids began.

During this period of the so-called phoney war, with no action on the Home Front, only those members of the staff who as Territorials had joined Hartley Cooper's own regiment, the Rifle Brigade, had been called up. So at Elstree we all settled down into a five-day period of work and play which I suspect made many of the younger members quite happy to return each Monday morning. The juniors were billeted in the Sports Pavilion of Haberdashers' Aske's School, some two miles from the offices, the girls slept in Summerfield House, and I was one of eight fortunate fellows who shared a flat overlooking Borehamwood Station, where coal and munition trains rumbled through all night. That winter was so cold in our unheated flat that we used to wake and brush the hoar frost off our blankets each morning.

It was business as usual, and plenty of it. Here is a typical working day in the Policy Office:

9 am – walk to office across the fields from our flat.

9.30 am to 1 pm – work.

1 to 2.30 pm – eat sandwiches, visit the Plough, Artichoke or Holly Bush, or take a walk to Aldenham Reservoir, the local beauty spot.

2.30 to 5.30 pm – work.

Then at 6 pm about a dozen of us gathered for an evening meal in the upstairs room of a nearby café, kept by a very plump young lady known disrespectfully but affectionately as Ma Sedgwick. She and her waitress did us proud.

7 pm – return to office to work until 10 pm. If we had any problems or urgent policy checking we popped down the road to the Saloon Bar of the Plough where our bosses, Harry Band and John Trendall, were happy to advise over their pints.

10 pm – back to the flat on the last bus, a game of darts, hot cocoa and bed.

As time went by we arranged social events. We challenged Bowrings to darts and dominoes, and I beat Bowrings domino champion in a match played on the set of a film in production in the studios. There were also the parties arranged by the girls in Summerfield House under the fatherly eye of Harry Hand, where in this large, rambling building we played "Murder". But more of that anon!

Tommy Tonkin

at Hartley Cooper, the firm's contribution to creating shelters in the Gracechurch Street building, and the provision of training in first aid for female staff – of whom, by then, there were perhaps a dozen, employed as typists and secretaries. On the outbreak of war, the back-up departments moved to rented premises at Elstree. Those left in London had to have their deferrals renewed every six months, and combined their working day with firewatching and the Home Guard. It was "business as usual" at Gracechurch Street and in the City, even with the advent of the terrifying V2 rockets in 1944. One young broker's impression of Lloyd's was that it was "like the Windmill: it never closed". If a big raid threatened, the Room was vacated in favour of a basement warren in which each underwriter had his cubbyhole; the broker's

Work continues in the basement of Lloyd's during an air raid in the Second World War.

challenge was to find the man he wanted in what was virtually a maze.

"I returned to a City utterly changed", one Hartley Cooper employee recalled, but although the physical environment had altered greatly, the firm had survived relatively unscathed and carried on its business much as it always had. One significant change, however, was to its legal status – from partnership to private limited company – as a result of having to comply with the Companies Act 1948. It was a welcome development since those staff shareholders who wished to sell their shares and retire could now do so more easily.

Into the Modern World

John Francis stands beside the plaque dedicated to his cousin, Francis Francis in Winchester Cathedral.

In the post-war economic climate, Hartley Cooper's links with the United States became even stronger, and trans-Atlantic travel on the firm's business much more common. Crossing the ocean on one of the *Queens* (or, in a few years, by air), then criss-crossing the continent by rail, became part of a senior broker's job. The firm acquired clients such as Alabama Dry Dock, based in Mobile, Alabama, but with depots all over the United States, and the Hawaii-based Dillingham Land, construction and railway interests, run from San Francisco. Largest of all was National Bulk Carriers, the marine freight company created by the reclusive but philanthropic Daniel K. Ludwig. Hartley Cooper were brokers to the London portion of this vast account, while the New York firm of Marsh McLennan, with which Hartley Cooper was on excellent terms, were brokers to the rest. National Bulk Carriers were one of several companies that pioneered the supertanker and the container-ship, initiating the decline of the traditional fleets of steamers that once carried goods to every corner of the globe, and of the shipyards that built them. Other clients at this time included Farrell Lines and Maryland Shipbuilding & Dry Dock Company in the U.S. In the U.K. a big client was Stephenson Clarke. The vast tankers and their cargoes represented far bigger and more concentrated risks than had ever required insurance before. Reinsurance, traditionally not an area in which Lloyd's had specialised to any great extent, soon became a growth area in response. Hartley Cooper was the first Lloyd's broker to design and use the A4 size "SG" Marine policy form in the 1970s.

Several important U.K. companies became Hartley Cooper clients soon after the war. One was the Martin-Baker Aircraft Company, whose proprietor, Sir James Martin, had already invented the prototype of the aircraft ejector seat. Years of testing and refinement would result in the production of a device that would become standard in military aircraft and save thousands of lives worldwide. Another two such clients were Harvey's of Bristol and Readers' Digest. All of these connections came about through the introduction of John Francis, Hartley Cooper's leading U.K. non-marine broker, whose social and business acquaintance (and that of his

Sir Winston Churchill, in ebullient form, attends the opening of Lloyd's new Lime Street building in 1958.

A cheque signed by Sir Winston to Hartley Cooper for insurance to cover personal effects.

Facing Page:
Brokers regard the Casualty Board at Lloyd's in the 1950s.

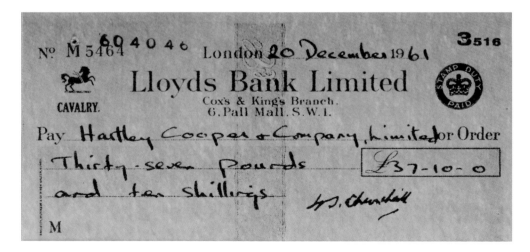

TELEGRAMS-NOT FOR PUBLICATION

NOTICE.

Life savers

Martin-Baker Aircraft Company Limited, formally incorporated in August 1934, was founded by James Martin (pictured), Valentine Baker and Francis Francis. Each of these men contributed their own unique gifts to the company: Martin provided his talent as an engineer and his passion for designing aeroplanes; Francis, a cousin of John Francis of Hartley Cooper, supplied the funds from the considerable fortune he had inherited from his grandfather; Baker contributed his flying skills, but sadly he died prematurely in September 1942 in a tragic accident while testing an aeroplane.

Despite Martin's passion for designing aircraft, it was his design of the ejection seat rather than his fighter aeroplanes that proved to be the great success story. He had become interested in the concept of a pilot's escape route from a jet as early as 1944, well before engineers in other countries had begun to develop it. There was some resistance from pilots to using an ejection seat because the early versions could result in twisted spines and broken bones, so Martin studied the human skeleton to see if he could limit such damage. He concluded that a series of timed detonations to power the seat, rather than a single big boost, would better protect pilots' backs, and so it proved.

Bernard Lynch, an employee of Martin-Baker who tested the seats for the company, suffered no injuries. He was ejected from a static seat in January 1945 and then, after a test with a dummy in flight in June 1946, he was ejected from a Gloster Meteor travelling at 320 mph at 8200 feet on 24 July 1946. It seems an extraordinarily brave thing to have done, but later evidence proved he was in safe hands since there have been no injuries to any of the pilots who have tested James Martin's prototypes. The method of timed boosts, along with the invention of

James Martin had become interested in the concept of a pilot's escape route from a jet as early as 1944.

seats which could eject safely on take-off or landing, was the key to his company's success and enabled it to win contracts with the U.S. Navy, which remains its biggest client to date.

Francis Francis's involvement with the company ended in the 1950s but his cousin John Francis continued to be involved, since Hartley Cooper provided all its insurance needs. Martin-Baker continued to grow and develop, and now the company is still family run by James Martin's twin sons John and James, with a staff of some 700 people, still based on a site in the sleepy English countryside, at Higher Denham, Buckinghamshire.

was saved by an ejection seat developed by Martin-Baker. The event was chalked up as the 7000th life saved by the company. According to its website, which provides a daily count of the number of lives it has saved, the current figure stands at over 7200 pilots who owe their lives to Martin-Baker.

Today HSBC Insurance Brokers – which absorbed Hartley Cooper – handles the company's employers' liability, public liability and some fire insurance. They also arrange insurance for the company's aeroplanes and motor fleet, goods in transit and travel, and organise engineering inspections. Martin-Baker has two old jets, one of which – a Meteor, built in the 1940s and used for ejection seat testing – is believed to be the oldest flying military jet in the world. These jets are delineated as military rather than civilian aircraft, because the special flying which is required in order to test the seats effectively (for instance flying at just 50 metres off the ground at Martin-Baker's Oxfordshire airfield) would not be permitted under civil aviation rules. HSBC's insurance covers hull risks and third party with an agreed value because the aircraft have vintage status.

Saving lives is Martin-Baker's business. When Commander Schwab, Lt Commander in the Royal Navy, baled out of his fighter jet spinning out of control off the English coastline in a routine test flight in June 2003, his life cousin Francis Francis, a champion golfer) was immense. John Francis was also the link to solicitors Fladgates of Pall Mall, through which Hartley Cooper came to broke insurance for four British prime ministers. The first was Sir Winston Churchill, whose cheque is still proudly preserved. The others – all of whom arranged insurance for jewellery and personal effects – were Sir Anthony Eden (later Earl of Avon), Sir Harold Macmillan (later Earl of Stockton) and Sir Edward Heath.

A significant activity not yet mentioned was the insurance of fine art through Hartley Cooper's associate Duveen & Walker, also based at 85 Gracechurch Street. Hartley Cooper had been placing the business of this small but prestigious company at Lloyd's for many years. It was formed by Captain Ernest Duveen, one of the six younger brothers of the great art dealer Sir Joseph (later Lord) Duveen; and William Walker, an architect influenced by the Arts and Crafts Movement. Captain Duveen (who survived a plane crash while serving in the Royal Flying Corps in 1916, and was still working at 86 in the mid-1950s) loved the art world, but sought to maintain a degree of independence from the family dynasty. Walker soon faded from the scene, but Duveen built up a thriving business through his personal acquaintance with the leading dealers in Paris, London and New York, and with some of the world's wealthiest collectors. His firm consisted of himself and his secretary, Miss Peggy Atkinson (later to be the first woman appointed as a director of a Hartley Cooper subsidiary), and insured not only individual works for private clients, but galleries, dealers' showrooms, exhibitions and artworks in transit. He was also a dealer on his own account. One retired member of staff remembers seeing a Picasso and a Modigliani among the paintings at the Captain's home. Another, who attended a gallery show where most of the works were insured by "D&W", observed to his companion that "£7 million on one wall" was something neither of them was likely to see again.

**Queen Elizabeth II attended the opening of
the new Lloyd's building in 1958.**

The reputation of Duveen & Walker was unrivalled in art circles between the wars. In 1946 however, they arranged the insurance of some invalid tricycles for the British Red Cross. This later led to the insurance of thousands of such vehicles for the then Ministry of Pensions and eventually for the organisation known as Motability. It was one of the largest blocks of motor insurance business yet written in the United Kingdom, worth some £40 million. From this point Duveen & Walker also began to be seen as a motor insurance broker as well as a broker of fine art insurance; both areas complemented the broking services offered by Hartley Cooper. After the death of Captain Duveen, Duveen & Walker was acquired by Hartley Cooper.

Through most of its history, Hartley Cooper has been a firm with an international outlook, thanks to its many clients in other continents. It was not surprising that it should be touched by world events far away, and so it was: in 1956, at the height of the Suez crisis. One of its marine clients, the Farrell Shipping Line, had a ship that was half-way through the Suez Canal when the crisis broke and was stalled there for the better part of a year. Not only did relief crews have to be flown out at intervals, but the unfortunate vessel's cargo of apples rapidly fermented in the heat. John East, the firm's leading "Hull" broker, had the delicate task of negotiating the ship's release.

Lloyd's had by this time taken advantage of wartime bomb damage to acquire a huge site on the other side of Lime Street and was constructing a new building. After five years, what became known as the "1958 building" was ready. Its royal opening was commemorated by the artist Terence Cuneo, and for the whole City financial community the building was indeed something to celebrate. The new Room was 100 yards long and equipped with a thoroughly modern electro-mechanical calling system that replaced the human "Caller" and made it easy for underwriters and brokers to make clear their whereabouts when summoned. Another novelty was the separation of the markets, with marine syndicates being located on the ground floor and non-marine syndicates in the gallery. The Committee room incorporated a salon by Robert Adam brought from Bowood House.

It was to this room that John East, by then Hartley Cooper's deputy Chairman, came when he took his seat on the Committee of Lloyd's in 1959 – the only broker up to that time, as opposed to underwriter, to be a Committee member. His duties included interviewing those who wished to become "Names". He was not at that point a Name himself, which may also have been unique, and certainly gave him a heightened sense of the gravity of what was being contemplated. At the conclusion of each interview, as the candidate reached the door, East would say in a sepulchral voice: "Don't forget – you will be liable down to your last shirt-button!" East remained on the Committee of Lloyd's until 1962, and served on it again from 1964 to 1971. Perhaps there were Names who recalled his words in the aftermath of Hurricane Betsy, or of any other disaster that resulted in "cash calls".

Church Brothers and other Acquisitions

The 1960s, in which the pace of change in every field of life seemed to accelerate, saw in the City the beginnings of the tendency towards the creation of larger and larger entities that still prevails today. The decade also witnessed the beginnings of the technological revolution. Both these developments were felt at Hartley Cooper. In the face of competition from larger, amalgamated firms of brokers, the directors were becoming aware of the need to strengthen the U.K. and non-marine sides of the business. In 1966 there arose an opportunity to do so, by acquiring Church Brothers – a small to medium-sized Lloyd's broker whose business nicely complemented Hartley Cooper's own.

It is hard for the office workers of the current era to imagine using the machinery of previous eras: these dictation machines were an innovation for typists in the 1960s.

An early version of Hartley Cooper's
open-plan policy office, on the fourth floor,
85 Gracechurch Street. In the late 1960s
computers are notable by their absence.

Church Brothers was founded in 1897 by F.W. Church, who was broker to much
of the woodworking and piano manufacturing industry and numbered the major
piano-makers among his clients. This gave him access to ancillary trades, such as
cabinet-making and fine metal wire-drawing, which was involved in making gold
and silver braid for military badges and medals. Church operated as a sole trader
until the 1930s, when he took two partners: Arthur Forrow and Charles Grint.

With the coming of war in 1939, Grint went into the forces. Church, by then eld-
erly, died in 1940, and Grint obtained a class B release to return to the business. Its
affairs were in a parlous state and over the next several years it was painstakingly
rebuilt. Once it was again viable, Grint bought out Church's heirs and later purchased Forrow's share, so that he became the business's sole proprietor. In time it

Disablement and Motability

Duveen & Walker, a division of Gibbs Hartley Cooper, were closely involved with the provision of transport for disabled people. They acted for the British Red Cross Society in the 1940s in insuring a small fleet of hand-propelled mackintosh-covered "invalid tricycles", at what Peggy Atkinson (secretary to Ernest Duveen) described as "5s a knob". When the National Health Service began in 1948, the then Ministry of Pensions consulted the Red Cross about insurance matters and it was that connection which led to Duveen & Walker arranging insurance for disabled drivers.

By the mid-1970s, although almost every household in the UK had a car, the help given to disabled people was very limited. Only those who could drive themselves could obtain some government support, which was primarily for a single-seater motor tricycle, which could not take passengers. Those people whose disabilities prevented them from driving received no state help and, for considerable numbers, this meant not being able to get out and about.

In 1976, the government introduced the Mobility Allowance, a sum of money which was given to those severely disabled people who were unable or virtually unable to walk, regardless of their ability to drive. For the first time, they were given financial help towards obtaining their own vehicle. However, although this was a great step forward, the sum of money offered was still insufficient to purchase even the smallest car, let alone one with any necessary adaptations.

The Government asked the late Lord Goodman to consider what might be done to help in partnership with business. He enlisted the key aid of

Peter Large, a governor of Motability, demonstrates the use of a Kartop hoist, which levers a disabled person out of a car, during the International Year of Disabled People, 8th June 1981.

Jeffrey Sterling, now Lord Sterling of Plaistow and current Chairman of Motability.

The scheme which emerged after consultation involved the combination of three necessary elements in providing

LPL 837P

suitable cars – the banks for finance, the four major UK motor manufacturers (supplying the cars) and the companies that would adapt the cars to meet the needs of the disabled people using them. The aim was to provide a car for the price of the disability benefit. The Motability Scheme began operating in 1978, with all-party support, and it proved to be a great success. It was formed as a charity, so that it could raise funds and make grants in order to be able to give customers a complete mobility package, even if their allowance did not entirely cover the type of car and kind of adaptation needed. It was a breakthrough in enabling people with a disability to live a normal life with the means of transport to jobs, shops and social events, and also the freedom to travel.

As the Motability Scheme grew, other manufacturers came on board and the six major U.K. clearing banks provided the necessary funding. The objectives were that disabled people should be able to afford to have a good-quality car from any participating manufacturer, and that they could acquire the car fully insured, serviced and with breakdown cover. By providing cars for disabled people, the scheme also facilitated the mobility of their wider families.

By 1984, Duveen & Walker arranged insurance for some 9500 Motability vehicles. The firm retained this considerable account right up to the time of the merger between Antony Gibbs and Hartley Cooper. Since the Motability Scheme began, over 2,000,000 cars, powered wheelchairs and scooters have been provided to disabled people to help meet their mobility needs.

The scheme began operating in 1978 under the name of Motability and it proved to be a great success.

became a limited partnership, with Grint and his three sons holding the stock, and two other working directors.

The 1950s were years of vigorous growth in every area of U.K. insurance business, and Church Brothers' offices in Queen Victoria Street were soon outgrown. The firm, with about 70 staff, moved to more spacious premises at Enfield. Its strength was in U.K. non-marine business, but it was also well run and highly profitable, at a time when many companies active in this field were, for a variety of reasons, losing money on U.K. business.

The acquisition of Church Brothers was the first step in a programme of expansion for Hartley Cooper. The idea was to broaden its base by acquiring smaller brokers with specialisations in areas where Hartley Cooper itself was not particularly strong. Since further acquisitions were expected, a legal and administrative umbrella company, Hartley Cooper (Holdings) was created. The newly merged U.K. non-marine entity made up of Hartley Cooper and Church Brothers was renamed Hartley Cooper Church.

Several other small U.K. companies were absorbed in the next few years. In 1976 Hartley Cooper bought J.R.W. Leiper, a brokerage based in Aberdeen with offices in Dundee, Elgin and Ayr. This business, founded by John Leiper in 1966, concentrated on life and pensions business but also had several large clients in the haulage industry. Hartley Cooper had recently entered into an agreement with Alexander & Alexander Inc. to handle the U.K. accounts of American companies placing their worldwide insurances through the New York firm. The Leiper acquisition allowed Hartley Cooper to do this more easily, and gave it a much-needed representation in Scotland and the north-east of England, although in time the other offices were closed and operations were centred on Aberdeen. Other businesses acquired were a Colchester-based warehousing business, W. Fieldgate, and J.H. Dewey of Claygate,

Surrey, a small non-Lloyd's brokerage that had been working closely with Hartley Cooper for some time. J.H. Dewey brought with it two subsidiaries, Dewey Warren (Home) Limited and Dewey Warren (Insurance Services) Limited. Two small general insurance broking firms were bought in 1982: Goddard & Goddard Ltd, and John W. Dunham & Partners Ltd. This also allowed the life and pensions business to expand.

Changing Times

The impression recalled by some retired Hartley Cooper staff, to the effect that "it suddenly all seemed to have become so much bigger", was no illusion. Hartley Cooper (Holdings) by 1972 was employing 286 people, 120 of them based at the former Church Brothers offices at Enfield where the U.K. business was now housed. The computer had definitely arrived, in the form of a gigantic IBM mainframe which was hoisted through a second-storey window at Gracechurch Street by a crane one Sunday morning in the late 1960s. (As it happened, the company reverted for a time to manual calculations when the computer-generated ones proved more expensive and less accurate than expected.) The working ethics and social mores of the City were shifting: the old, accepted standards of trust, the belief that a man's word was his bond, and the close network of professional acquaintance were all under pressure. Times were indeed changing, with what sometimes felt like alarming rapidity.

In 1972, a solution was found to the perennial problem of how to free up shares in Hartley Cooper (Holdings) for those who wanted to realise their shareholdings. The firm's old associate, Chubb Corporation, took a 25 per cent interest in it, after considering the benefits of acquiring a first-hand presence in the London market. This

Saving the
safe deposits

When customers entrust their most precious items to a bank for safe keeping in a deposit box, they do so precisely because they are concerned about security in their homes. The onus is therefore very heavy on the bank in question to provide the expected security and, if a raid does occur, to return missing goods or provide compensation promptly. For the insurers, speedy and helpful reactions are of the essence to maintain the best of relations with *their* clients, but they must balance these against the need to ensure that a bank's customers are being honest in their claims – and it is notoriously difficult to be certain what is contained in a safe deposit box.

In order to raid a deposit box centre successfully, robbers need knowledge of the layout and the location of the vault, as well as familiarity with the procedures for access to the boxes, so it is therefore common for the raiders to have inside help, either through staff or through

people who have serviced the buildings. Insurers of safe deposit boxes operate an infidelity clause, which in effect negates a claim if it can be proven that a member of the deposit centre's staff is a culprit in a raid.

There have been a number of spectacular safe deposit robberies over the years, but the two which have most affected HSBC Insurance Brokers were the raids on Bank of America's safe deposit boxes in 1975 and on the

Knightsbridge Safe Deposit Centre in July 1987. Both these raids involved clients who were well experienced in arranging insurance for financial institutions.

The Bank of America had a separate safe deposit policy with the firm at the time of the raid on its depository in Davies Street, London, in April 1975. This type of policy was comparatively unusual, because the risk of such raids was generally considered to be

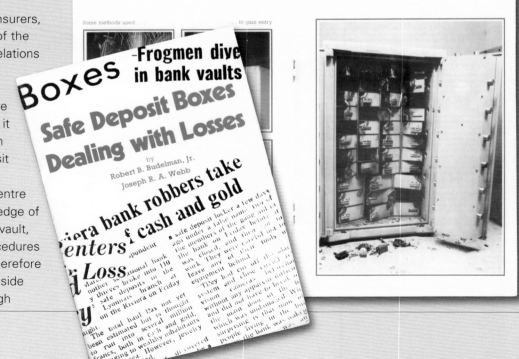

insignificant. However this case was so high profile, with the initial statement of losses put at £10 million, that it changed opinions. The New York law firm of Bigham Englar Jones & Houston were instructed to act on behalf of Hartley Cooper, and Bob Budelman, a resident partner in the firm, set up an office with the appointed Bank of America representative, Joseph R.A. Webb, a vice-president of the bank in London, to handle the losses. Nearly 100 box holders were interviewed and, with help from jewellery valuers and outside investigators, a settlement of some £5 million was made. Clients who could

the industry. With this experience, Bob Budelman and Joseph Webb wrote a booklet entitled *Safe Deposit Boxes: Dealing with Losses*, which was published by Hartley Cooper in 1981 and printed in a second edition by Gibbs Hartley Cooper in 1984. It covered the way in which losses were incurred, the problems of ascertaining exactly what the losses were and how to go about investigating claims. In this way, Gibbs Hartley Cooper played a leading role in defining the handling of safe deposit claims.

The Knightsbridge Safe Deposit raid was world famous for the scale of the

A customer checks the contents of his safe deposit box.

Clients who could prove what had been in their boxes received 100 per cent of their claims.

prove what had been in their boxes received 100 per cent of their claims.

The matter took ten years to settle finally, but in the end the Bank of America was so impressed with the way in which Hartley Cooper had tackled the problem that they appointed them as their London brokers in respect of bankers blanket bond cover. In fact, the way in which the insurance claim was handled was considered a test case in

goods stolen. It took place in London on 12 July 1987 when two men, posing as well-dressed businessmen, entered the centre and asked if they could rent a deposit box. After they were shown to the vault, they threatened the manager and security guards with hand guns before opening the door to accomplices. Most of the safe deposit boxes were broken into and the gang left with a hoard estimated to be worth

between £40 million and £66 million at the time.

Police investigations proved that a senior manager of the centre was implicated in the robbery and he was duly sent to prison. In terms of insurance, the fact that an inside person had been involved invoked the infidelity clause in the underwriter's policy. Fortunately the police recovered a good deal of the stolen property.

had not been possible until the relaxation of the Lloyd's regulations on the foreign ownership of Lloyd's brokers in 1971. Smaller interests were subsequently sold to the South British Insurance Company (23%), another longstanding associate, and to the City merchant bank Robert Fleming & Co. (19%).

As though to bring some metaphorical wheel full circle, this was also an era of truly audacious criminal activity directed against the American banks. Gangs in the United States now employed every technological advance and were often successful to the tune of millions of dollars. In 1975 thieves struck farther afield, in London, at the Safe Deposit Company owned by Hartley Cooper's client, the Bank of America, in Davies Street, Mayfair. The haul on that occasion was £10 million in jewellery and cash. The thieves gained access to bank clients' safety deposit boxes after an accomplice had memorised the combination of the safe lock. This crime highlighted

Hartley Cooper's cricket team in 1978.
Pictured from left to right:
Geoffrey Shepheard, Roger Bassett, Tony
Eist, John Byrne, David Hampson, Ron Wood,
John Barnett and Chris Tanous (guest;
Mallard Communications).
In front kneeling: John Adams, Simon
Woodcock and Martin Waller.

From left to right: Tom Bland (deputy chairman), John East (chairman) and Ron Brazier (company secretary) in 1972 when Chubb purchased a shareholding in Hartley Cooper.

a glaring loophole in bank security. Depositors were not required to declare the contents of their boxes at the time of renting them, and this meant that the bank did not know what was stored in its vaults. The problem arose, in this instance, because the Bank of America did not wish to challenge depositors' claims after the event, and underwriters were unwilling to pay out on unsubstantiated claims. For its part, Hartley Cooper felt an obligation to help settle the claims in a manner acceptable to both. Thanks to the efforts of Robert Budelman, a partner in the New York law firm of Bigham Englar Jones & Houston briefed by underwriters to handle the claim, procedures were devised for determining the value of items lost and settlement was eventually reached for just under £5 million, to the satisfaction of all parties. Budelman and Joseph Webb later gathered their experiences into a booklet entitled *Safe Deposit Boxes: Dealing With Losses* which was published by Hartley Cooper in 1981 as a service to banks.

If recession and a series of natural disasters made the early 1970s a generally difficult time for the insurance industry, the period from 1975 to 1978 was exactly the opposite, as the world economy revived. In the words of one commentator on those years, "a flood of insurance business poured across the Atlantic into the London market". By 1980 this brief bonanza was over. A sudden wave of new initiatives seeking to cash in on the profitability of insurance produced fierce competition. In 1981 a new company, Hartley Cooper & Warner, was formed to enable high street brokers to have bulk access to the Lloyd's syndicates writing motor and other insurance business. It acted as guarantor to some 2000 non-Lloyd's brokers, taking a small commission payment against the risk of a broker's failure. This business proved both successful and highly profitable during what was about to become the most trying period of Hartley Cooper's existence.

In the previous decade, a number of American insurance businesses had purchased shareholdings in Lloyd's brokers – as Chubb had, in Hartley Cooper. Ostensibly this was done to enable them to participate in the brokerage earned on their insurance placed at Lloyd's, which could only be handled by Lloyd's brokers. The underlying reason, however, was the Lloyd's brokers' international spread of business, which would have been too expensive to compete for from scratch and which was highly attractive at a time when the North American market was so competitive.

With the abrupt change in conditions in the London market, the community of some 200 Lloyd's brokers, some very large, others very small, experienced a marked shift in favour of the largest entities. The Fisher Report of 1980 indicated that even in 1978 (the most recent year for which information was available) some 41 per cent of the total brokered premiums placed in all markets was placed by three firms – Sedgwicks, Bowrings and Willis Faber – and 68 per cent of total premiums were placed by only twelve. By 1982 the medium-sized Hartley Cooper was being squeezed by market conditions. The only way to maintain its position appeared to be growth through amalgamation along the lines already adopted, but on a much more ambitious scale.

It was in the autumn of that year that the seemingly unthinkable occurred: a major shareholder and client of Hartley Cooper announced its intention of moving its account to a much larger competitor. While a defection of such magnitude initially produced consternation, it was not long before some creative thinking was brought to bear. Over the next several months the options available were explored by the Hartley Cooper board and the other large shareholders. By the spring of 1983, the best course of action seemed to be a merger with another Lloyd's broker of similar size and complementary activities – but which? Appropriately enough, given the traditional ways of the City, it was the goodwill built up over the years that brought forward the right suitor at the right time.

Joining the HSBC Group

ENTER, THE HONGKONG AND SHANGHAI BANKING CORPORATION

Back in 1973, when Antony Gibbs & Sons Ltd. became a public limited company known as Antony Gibbs Holdings Ltd., a 20 per cent shareholding in it had been acquired by The Hongkong and Shanghai Banking Corporation (HSBC). Speaking of the Gibbs firm, the then Chairman of HSBC, Guy Sayer, indicated the importance of this acquisition in his statement in the 1973 annual report: "They are an old and respected name in the City and we look forward to working closely with them to our mutual benefit." A year later this stake was increased to 40 per cent. This new and important relationship came at a time when both entities were seeking to expand. Antony Gibbs Holdings needed to compete more effectively, and HSBC wished to enhance its presence in the City of London. In purchasing an interest in a merchant bank that was also an accepting house, it acquired not only a presence, but prestige and an entrée into one of the City's best-guarded inner circles.

The financial institution that now assumed such an important role in the life of the Antony Gibbs group of companies was itself the product of more than a century of colourful history. Founded in 1865, its original aim was to finance trade in the Far East, operating on sound "Scottish banking principles". The men who established it were committed to local ownership, and persuaded the Treasury in London to allow incorporation under a special Hong Kong ordinance. This enabled the bank to have its head office in Hong Kong, rather than London, without losing the privilege of issuing banknotes and holding government funds. It rapidly built up a network of agents and branches around the globe, but its main focus was on China and the rest of the Asia-Pacific region. By the turn of the century, it was the foremost financial institution in Asia.

In addition to the financing of trade, it had an international reputation that grew out of its role as banker to Governments, issuer of banknotes and manager of new loans. The bank's widespread presence in Asia, and especially in China, made it vulnerable to the catastrophes of war and civil war in the 20th century. By 1955 its branches in mainland China, with the exception of those in Shanghai, had been closed and the bank had taken on a key role in the reconstruction of the post-war Hong Kong economy.

It also began to diversify, through a series of acquisitions. Among these were The British Bank of the Middle East (1959), formerly the Imperial Bank of Persia, which had been established in London in 1889; Mercantile Bank (also 1959), dating from 1853 in Bombay, India; a controlling interest in Hang Seng Bank (1965) of Hong Kong, founded in 1933; and the formation of a merchant banking subsidiary, Wardley Limited, in 1972. A preliminary foray into banking in the United States in 1955 led to the acquisition in 1980 of a 51 per cent stake in Marine Midland Bank, Inc., which was based in New York State (Marine Midland would become wholly owned in 1987).

A London office of HSBC was opened within months of the bank's formation in 1865, but its headquarters was still located in Hong Kong. Both the Mercantile Bank and The British Bank of the Middle East had London offices, but by the late 1970s the parent company's strategy was to become sole owner of a City-based merchant bank with an international presence and a wide spectrum of involvements. Antony Gibbs Holdings Ltd fitted this bill well, and complemented the purchaser's existing banking interests.

The financial state of Antony Gibbs Holdings Ltd was not at this point robust,

HSBC's innovative headquarters, Hong Kong

The Hongkong and Shanghai Banking Corporation, now known as HSBC, set up its headquarters in Hong Kong in 1865, in a building known as Wardley House which stood on the bank's current site. This building was demolished in 1886 and the new construction, representing HSBC's growth, was designed as two almost separate buildings, with Victorian style colonnades fronting on One Queen's Road Central looking across Statue Square, and an arcade blending in with its neighbours in the adjacent Des Voeux Road. HSBC's next building on the same site was constructed in 1935 with contemporary design and standards in the fashionable and tall Chicago style. It was the first building in Hong Kong to be air conditioned.

By the 1970s, HSBC had completely outgrown this building and so the decision was taken in 1978 to demolish it and start again from scratch. Norman Foster designed the new building with Wimpey constructing it. Work on the site began in 1979 and the new building was completed six years later, in 1985. During this same period, the old Lloyd's building in London was also demolished to make way for Richard Roger's controversial modern building, which still stands today. These two buildings, HSBC's and Lloyd's, were considered innovative icons of their time.

The insurance cover for HSBC's project was especially complicated to arrange. The project was extremely ambitious, and at a cost of £500 million (HK$5.2 billion) it was the most expensive construction project in the world at that time. Segments of the

Some 30,000 tonnes of steel and 4500 tonnes of aluminium had to be brought in by ship.

building had to be built abroad and then shipped to Hong Kong to be assembled on site. The building consisted of five modules, all of which were prefabricated in Scotland by Scott-Lithgow Shipbuilders: some 30,000 tonnes of steel and 4500 tonnes of aluminium were required for construction and had to be brought in by ship. In order to provide cooling water for the air conditioning, a tunnel of some seven and a half metres in diameter had to be built underground to bring in water from the harbour. The tunnelling caused the land on one side of the Star Ferry terminal to sink and a French company had to be brought in to correct the problem. HSBC Insurance Brokers in Hong Kong sought reinsurance support for the construction and the risk was placed across several markets in London, the U.S. and Asia.

This third HSBC building stands at 180 metres with 47 storeys and 4 basement levels. The building remained in its original design until a new, prestigious lobby, designed by Greg Pearce to blend in with the original building, was added in 2006 with a multi-media installation of 30 plasma screens displaying archived material of HSBC's history and art.

and was judged to need stronger management. HSBC's purchase of the outstanding 60 per cent shareholding in 1980 was therefore a welcome development, and a mutually beneficial transaction. HSBC acquired as a subsidiary the merchant bank it had sought, while Antony Gibbs Holdings gained as a parent a diverse and powerful financial institution. The only sour note came with the not-unexpected withdrawal of the merchant bank's membership of the Accepting Houses Committee. This was because the bank was now deemed to be controlled from abroad.

HSBC also, of course, gained a Lloyd's broker with wide connections and experience, while Antony Gibbs, Sage was itself at a point where the need to grow had become paramount. HSBC's initial investments in Antony Gibbs Holdings had been made at a time when insurance broking was entering a promising phase. After several years (1975 to 1978) during which the insurance industry had enjoyed a kind of "golden age", conditions changed in 1979, as has already been mentioned. Intense new competition across the industry coincided with higher interest rates, higher brokers' expenses and falls in premium income and commission. Only the largest Lloyd's brokers could weather such a storm; the medium-sized businesses like Antony Gibbs, Sage Limited – not to mention the smaller entities with greater exposure in fewer areas – suffered greatly. The £776,000 profit gained in the heady days of 1976 had become a £1,004,000 loss by 1980.

Immediately after HSBC's acquisition of Antony Gibbs Holdings, Gibbs Sage (as Antony Gibbs, Sage was renamed) was given a welcome injection of £2.6 million of new capital. It could now embark on the overdue and thorough review and renewal of systems that were necessary if the two sides of the business, the Gibbs side and the Sage side, were to become fully integrated – a prerequisite for more efficient functioning, and for future growth.

The Acquisition of Hartley Cooper

As a member of such a large financial and services group, Gibbs Sage now had access to a vast international network of connections. A corporate plan from the early 1980s indicates that it continued to offer a full insurance broking service in all the major classes of insurance, but was also expected to provide a complete insurance service for any member company or client of HSBC.

But more immediately, it could plan confidently for the future – indeed, to justify itself as an investment, it *had* to plan for the future – in a manner that would overcome the difficulties inherent in its medium size. Gibbs Sage ranked 24th in terms of brokerage income among U.K. insurance brokers when its parent company was acquired by HSBC. Without substantial further investment, increasing its market share looked doubtful. That same corporate plan already mentioned set out a list of objectives – the first of which was the acquisition of a fellow Lloyd's broker of similar size. Gibbs Sage was thus already seeking such a partner at the point when it was introduced to Hartley Cooper Holdings, which was in a similar situation, in May 1983.

Both firms were at this point caught up in changing legislation, the result of which enhanced the prospect of their coming together. The Lloyd's Act of 1982 – significant because it heralded the beginning of the modern Lloyd's as a more closely regulated and accountable organisation – required Lloyd's brokers to divest themselves of managing agencies that controlled underwriting syndicates. The rationale behind this part of the Act was obvious: no broker should be able to control underwriting philosophy at the expense of fair and open competition.

Gibbs Sage at this point owned a managing agency which controlled two of the market's most profitable syndicates, one marine and one non-marine. Divestment came as a blow, since a stream of income to the overall business was lost once the managing agency was sold. Hartley Cooper was in much the same position, having also owned a small Names agency. Combining the two businesses was viewed as a one-step means of creating a broader palette of services, achieving economies of scale, and partially offsetting the loss of income resulting from the sale of the respective agencies.

This was only one of the reasons that made the match between Gibbs Sage and Hartley Cooper so clearly right for both firms that little time was needed for deliberation. By mid-July, HSBC and Antony Gibbs Holdings had given the acquisition their blessing, and agreement on the terms of an offer for the whole of the share capital of Hartley Cooper Holdings had been reached. Hartley Cooper's three major shareholders and its directors, whose interests together comprised 69.9 per cent of the existing issued share capital, had already accepted the offer by the time it was made in August to the remaining shareholders, mainly staff and retired employees. As the offer document spelled out, the proposed acquisition was being made "having particular regard to the complementary nature of the businesses…and the increasingly competitive international insurance market which is dominated to a great extent by a small number of large insurance broking groups". The respective businesses of Gibbs Sage and Hartley Cooper were to be "combined and developed in a single company to be called Gibbs Hartley Cooper Limited" so that their joint resources and expertise could be put towards a greater range of products and improved standards of service. What was being proposed was a synergistic move in which the resulting whole would be greater than the sum of the parts. The offer was overwhelmingly accepted, and by September 1983 Hartley Cooper Holdings had been formally acquired.

The acquisition also fitted neatly into HSBC's aim of expanding its insurance

By mid-July 1983, HSBC and Antony Gibbs Holdings had agreed to acquire the whole of the share capital of Hartley Cooper Holdings.

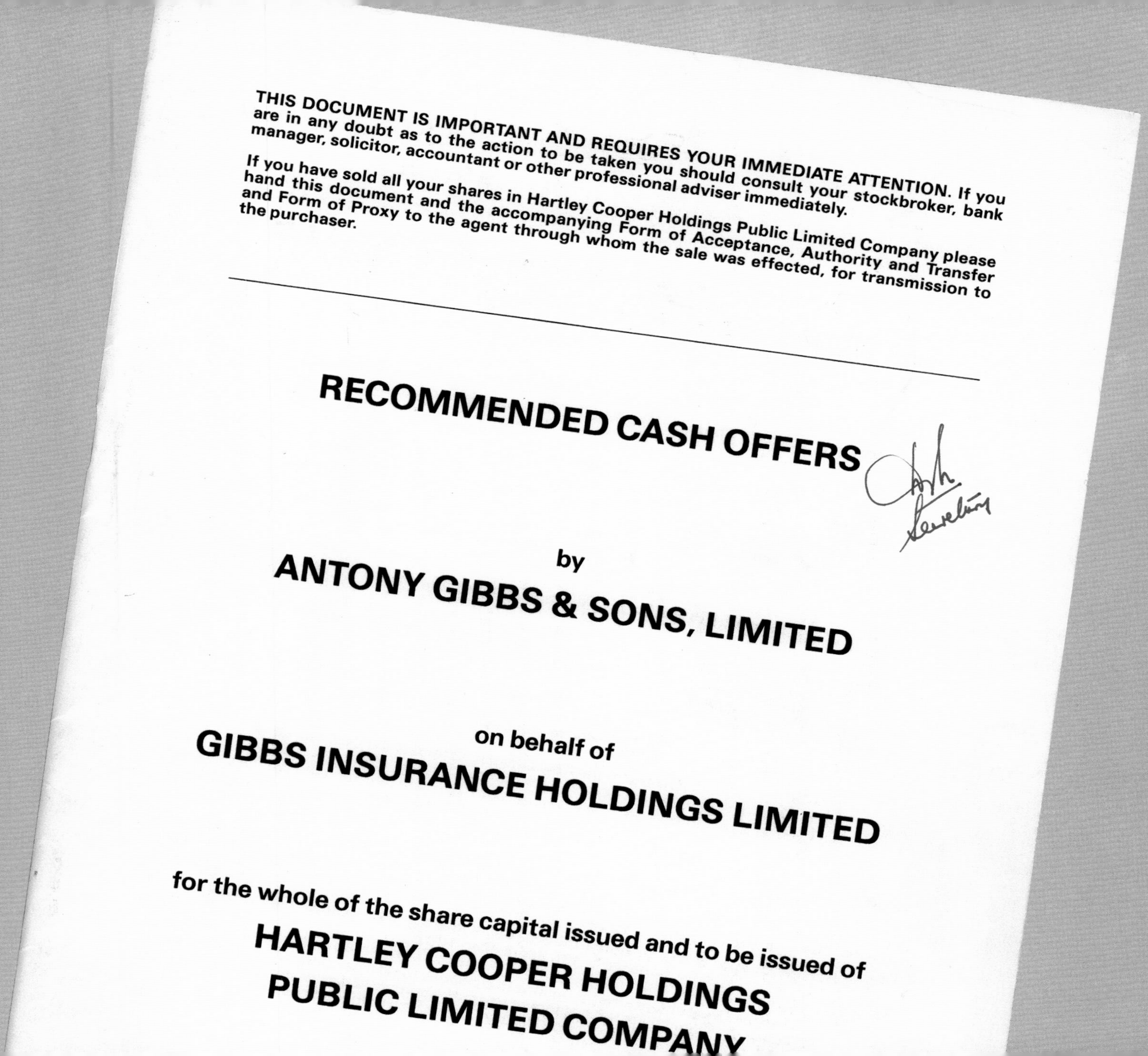

THIS DOCUMENT IS IMPORTANT AND REQUIRES YOUR IMMEDIATE ATTENTION. If you are in any doubt as to the action to be taken you should consult your stockbroker, bank manager, solicitor, accountant or other professional adviser immediately.

If you have sold all your shares in Hartley Cooper Holdings Public Limited Company please hand this document and the accompanying Form of Acceptance, Authority and Transfer and Form of Proxy to the agent through whom the sale was effected, for transmission to the purchaser.

RECOMMENDED CASH OFFERS

by

ANTONY GIBBS & SONS, LIMITED

on behalf of

GIBBS INSURANCE HOLDINGS LIMITED

for the whole of the share capital issued and to be issued of

HARTLEY COOPER HOLDINGS
PUBLIC LIMITED COMPANY

broking activities, which were an integral part of the range of financial services it provided worldwide. The merged company would rank 14th among the U.K. brokers, with brokerage income estimated at about £9 million. The new company's combined income was expected to exceed the operating cost of servicing its enlarged client base. At the same time, this larger client base would make the company more resilient to the loss of any single account, however important.

The Aim: Unity

Despite the many advantages and similarities highlighted by the acquisition, the merging of the two businesses was not without its cultural tensions. These were perhaps inevitable, and sprang largely from personality clashes, differences in management style and systems incompatibilities. Inevitably, material costs were high and the pressures to reduce them strong. There were some redundancies in the few areas where departments overlapped, and some resignations at senior level in the course of settling down. Initially the newly created subsidiary was headed by two directors from the former Gibbs Sage and two from the former Hartley Cooper, under a non-executive Chairman based in Hong Kong. The benefits of a more hands-on approach were quickly realised, however, and a London-based executive Chairman was appointed, with a brief to unify and consolidate the company.

At the time of the offer, Hartley Cooper had already been intending a move from its long-term headquarters at 85 Gracechurch Street. The rapidly executed amalgamation made it imperative to find new premises large enough to house most of the combined staff of Gibbs Hartley Cooper, numbering roughly 500. In due course a lease was taken on Bishops Court, a modern building of striking design located in

HSBC Insurance Brokers has for many years supported the annual music festival that takes place at Christ Church, Spitalfields, built by Nicholas Hawksmoor in 1720.

HSBC Insurance Brokers moved into Bishops Court, Spitalfields in 1983, one of the first new office buildings to be built in the area since the Second World War and heralding the new office blocks to come in the area in the late 1990s.

Artillery Lane, on the edge of Spitalfields. This was an area rich in history. Gibbs Hartley Cooper employees soon became aware that recent archaeological digs had uncovered finds dating back to Roman times, while the ruins of the former priory and hospital of St Mary Spital proclaimed the importance of the site in the Middle Ages. While the name Bishops Court was a modern appellation, Artillery Lane commemorated the centuries when the "Fraternyte or Guylde of Artyllary of Longbowes, Crossebowes and Handgonnes" had used the open space adjacent to the priory as a practice ground. Later, after the dissolution of the monasteries, it was used by the trained bands of the City of London and the gunners from the Tower to perfect their skills.

In 1983, the area was still undeveloped. Spitalfields Market to the north still functioned on five days a week and Bishops Court was one of the first modern office blocks constructed east of Bishopsgate since 1945. Today – a quarter of a century later, and despite competition from newer buildings nearby – its novel design continues to prompt admiring comments. Five storeys high, the white-painted steel structure is arranged around a spacious interior atrium, through whose glass roof the daylight pours. A glass-sided lift offers the best view of this attractive feature. In an open court below ground level, trees, stones and a pool containing carp provide a calm oasis reminiscent of a Zen garden. It is probably no exaggeration to suggest that the building aided the merger of cultures in Gibbs Hartley Cooper: everyone was proud of it and pleased to work in an environment that visually reinforced the ideas of openness and clarity. It was also fun: hardly had the company taken up residence than the first of many commercial film crews was on site, attracted by a "space-age" architecture then almost unique in the City.

By 1986, in the wake of financial deregulation of the London Stock Exchange – the so-called "Big Bang" that reverberated through the entire financial community – Gibbs Hartley Cooper had emerged from its period of adjustment as a leaner, better organised company. Small teams of experts had been recruited and offered equity stakes in newly created subsidiaries, with the aim of expanding certain areas of the business. A core computer system had been installed, and for the first time personnel systems and training programmes were in place. An unprofitable division, Bloodstock, was closed down in 1987, along with the North American operation established years before by Lionel Sage. Strengthening the reinsurance area, or Treaty department, had become a priority. The experts brought into this area were encouraged to use the most advanced modelling and analytical techniques to build it up. As this was virtually a new department, a prime objective was to achieve

The atrium at Vintners' Place, a new office into which over 200 staff moved in February 2008.

The atrium at Bishop's Court and the long-lived carp that are so beloved of the staff.

credibility in the market. This it quickly did, gaining major clients such as Migdal in Israel and Prudential in the U.K., and many others in the Caribbean, the Middle East and the Far East.

Reinsurance is a global business, with clients located all over the world, but especially in the wide band around the equator which is so prone to natural disasters. In the event of typhoon, flood or other catastrophe, the reinsurer's immediate and sometimes most important role is to provide a client with moral support. To one client, facing devastating losses after experiencing two hurricanes in ten days, it made all the difference to find that the Treaty department had wired him a cheque for £10 million with which to start paying claims, even before he had been able to request it.

Natural disasters such as this typhoon are part and parcel of the global reinsurance business.

New Additions

Despite a dramatic increase in overheads in the City and a falling U.S. dollar (which had a negative impact on North American business), the mid-1980s were once again good years for Lloyd's brokers, with dramatic rises in premium rates and in profits. Yet Gibbs Hartley Cooper was still small in terms of the overall market, and hindered, like so many brokers of its size, by a lack of specialisation. A good deal of analysis was already going into identifying likely candidates to which future offers to purchase might be made. What the company most needed was to acquire a number of small brokers whose main activities neatly filled the empty niches in its own range.

This need was felt even more acutely when in 1987 HSBC purchased a 14.9 per cent shareholding in the Midland Bank, one of the U.K.'s largest clearing banks. (Prior to acquiring the rest of the Midland in 1992, a new holding company, HSBC Holdings plc, was created. To comply with U.K. regulations, the group's head office was transferred from Hong Kong to London early in 1993.) From about the same time, Gibbs Hartley Cooper embarked upon the route already suggested for it by purchasing some specialised businesses.

The first of these was the U.K. division of Frizzell, one of the country's leading retail brokers, in 1991. The history of the parent company, founded as Norman Frizzell & Partners in 1923 (though at that time the enterprising young Glaswegian had no partners) offers an example of how far a good idea can go when backed by vision and drive. Frizzell began as a general broker, but when he acquired the account of the Civil Service Motoring Association, he suddenly grasped the similarity of the individual members as a group, and conceived the idea of what today would be called "affinity group" marketing. From insurance for the CSMA

A long association

Exchem, part of the EPC Groupe, based in Paris, was established in the U.K. in 1905 as Explosives and Chemical Products Limited, having acquired an existing licensed explosives factory in Essex. In the early 1950s, the company set up a second site in Derbyshire, its initial purpose being to receive products from the Essex site which were sent there to be finished and distributed. The company also established two farms, to form protected areas around the two factories.

By the 1960s, the site in Derbyshire had begun to manufacture a key component of many explosives products made at that time. This strategy was so successful that by 1981 it was producing explosives based on nitroglycerine at the rate of 7500 tonnes a year. The products were used both in the U.K. and abroad in deep coal mines, quarries and tunnelling work.

A new plant came into operation in Derbyshire in December 1983, producing a water-gel or "slurry" explosive. Initially, the rate of production was 2 tonnes per hour, but progress was rapid, and this figure increased to 3 tonnes per hour by 1986 and subsequently to 4 tonnes per hour. At the height of its capacity, the plant was producing 5500 tonnes per annum. By 1985 the company had switched all its explosives production to Derbyshire, and from then on the Essex site concentrated on the production of fuel additives and speciality chemicals. In 1990 a complex of new buildings and plant was added to the Derbyshire operations, with the objective of providing customers with a complete explosives service. The new facilities incorporated the ability to manufacture

Exchem's insurances have been placed through Richards Longstaff, now part of HSBC Insurance Holdings, since the 1950s.

detonating cord and to assemble detonators.

In the early 1990s, a new plant was built at the site to produce emulsion matrix, a step that had far reaching implications for the way in which explosives were used. This particular substance only became an explosive when mixed with other ingredients at the sites where blasting was required – such as quarries and open-cast coal-mining sites. This removed many of the concerns associated with transporting conventional explosives. Exchem commissioned its own "Multiblend" trucks to transport the materials to the point of usage. The final link in the service chain was completed with the purchase of drilling and blasting companies that were already well established. Thus Exchem could offer its customers a complete package, including the use of its own rigs to drill the shot holes in quarries to take the explosives. The development of its emulsion matrix was a significant breakthrough for the explosives division. By December 2000 the nitroglycerine plant, and associated mixing and packing buildings, had been shut, and they were decommissioned two years later.

Exchem's insurances have been placed through Richards Longstaff, now part of HSBC Insurance Holdings, since the 1950s. They have provided all the company's necessary cover on manufacturing plant and for the farms, excluding liability, for over 50 years. Three of the HSBC Insurance Brokers team who cover this area of business at Vintners' Place have been involved with Exchem over a period of 17 years, seeing the company through all its various stages of change and evolution.

members' cars, he went on to offer them insurance on their homes, the contents, and travel. Over the next 50 years, as the CSMA membership increased to some half-million, the Frizzell firm grew with it. It also acquired the business of other group clients: the General and Municipal Workers' Union and the National Union of Teachers, among others. The company was active in commercial and life and pensions areas too, but it was on the core area of providing insurance for groups that its success was really built. It prided itself on personal service and transparency, and on a stable of loyal clients, such as Hall & Woodhouse, Shaftesbury plc, Cheshire Homes and the Court of Protection.

Despite – or perhaps because of – its success, by the late 1980s Frizzell was vulnerable to a takeover. The major shareholder – the Frizzell family – decided to sell while this could still be done with a degree of independence. At the time when the U.K. side of the business was bought by Gibbs Hartley Cooper, it employed some 2000 people. Although there were some redundancies, on the whole the transaction went smoothly and the Frizzell regional offices – in Manchester, Birmingham, Newcastle, Poole and London – were integrated into the network of Gibbs Hartley Cooper locations.

The second of the acquisitions was Richards Longstaff (Holdings) Ltd in 1993. Founded in 1928, the firm had been a Lloyd's broker until 1933, but ceased to be so on entering into working associations with John Poole & Sons Ltd. Later, it merged with Wright Deen & Co. Ltd, run by Col. Percy Wright and Maurice Deen (founder of the Blue Star garage chain). Richards Longstaff regained its status as an independent Lloyd's broker in 1974 when a management buyout brought about a reconstruction in which the original business joined with the U.K. business of Wright, Deen & Co. to create Richards Longstaff (Holdings) Ltd.

While Richards Longstaff also handled marine, overseas, and pensions business,

Part of Richards Longstaff's aviation division arranged insurance for hot-air balloons, covering 40 per cent of this market in the U.K. as well as abroad.

the areas that were of greater interest to Gibbs Hartley Cooper were its Aviation and Estates departments. Richards Longstaff provided cover for a range of aircraft, from museum pieces to modern record breakers, private planes and helicopters. It was also the leading broker of insurance for hot-air balloons, with 40 per cent of this specialised market in the U.K., as well as a substantial amount of international business. Gibbs Hartley Cooper's own small Aviation division concentrated heavily on the insurance requirements of aerospace manufacturers, so that there was virtually no overlap when the two divisions came together.

The Estates business, which had begun in a small way as part of a non-marine department, had gradually turned Richards Longstaff into the most trusted name in a specialised field. Supplying the insurance needs of what amounted to a roll-call of Britain's landowners, many of them titled, demanded a detailed and personalised service, as well as continuity, discretion and absolute trust. Among the estates for which insurance matters were handled were the Castle of Mey, Woburn Abbey, the Compton and the Duke of Norfolk's estates, Bramham Park and Berkeley Castle, and there was a host of others. The usual request was cover for valuable contents such as paintings, silver, furniture and carpets. The broker's annual visit to each client required him to be knowledgeable, observant and attentive rather than overly admiring or awe-struck, whatever he was shown. Items had to be very fully and precisely described so that the right amount of insurance could be calculated and the underwriter's desire for detailed information satisfied.

The insurance of estates was not an area in which Gibbs Hartley Cooper was already represented, and Richards Longstaff's uniquely successful estates area was therefore a welcome addition. The third and last acquisition, that of the Holmwoods Group in 1995, also brought Gibbs Hartley Cooper a completely new area of expertise, schools insurance. This company existed from 1840, when C. Holmwood began

Richards Longstaff covered insurance for a number of estates in the U.K. including the Castle of Mey, which was owned by Queen Elizabeth the Queen Mother.

underwriting at Lloyd's. Under the guidance of his son Thomas Holmwood, the Insurance department of Holmwood & Holmwood (by then a merchant bank) merged with that of Back & Manson in 1920. The latter supplied iron and steel for bridge and railway construction, and had an insurance department that dated from 1913. As Holmwoods & Back & Manson, the new firm survived the turbulent 1920s to prosper as a Lloyd's broker, with its own syndicates handling marine and non-marine business.

It was in 1926 that Holmwoods & Back & Manson set up a Schools division under the guidance of Alec Dewar, who was advisor to the Private Schools Association. He had identified a gap in the market and devised the Schools Fees Remission Scheme, the forerunner of today's School Fees Protection Scheme, to fill it. (This scheme provided for the return of a proportion of fees to parents if a child were taken ill or died.) With a colleague, Leslie Langton, who advised the Association of Preparatory Schools, a specialisation was built up that soon made the company Britain's market leader in schools insurance broking. Dewar subsequently exported his schemes to the United States, where they enjoyed great success.

In 1974 Holmwoods was acquired by the Brown Shipley Group, and merged with a fellow Lloyd's broker dating from 1883, Crawfurd Beck & Amos, which was also owned by Brown Shipley. The business of Crawfurd Beck & Amos related mainly to marine cargoes. In the 1930s the company began to specialise in broking insurance for international businesses managed from London: largely mining and commodities concerns in Asia, Africa and Australia. For many years it was unique in placing in the London market the workman's compensation insurance applicable in many former colonial countries. The widespread unrest that characterised some of these areas after the Second World War made this a difficult business to sustain. By the 1960s, the independence of some nations and adverse political conditions in others

Thomas D. Holmwood joined the original firm of Holmwood & Row, founded by his father Charles Holmwood, in 1861 and became both a member of Lloyd's and an underwriter in that year. In 1902 the firm of Holmwood & Holmwood became a limited company.

**The Holmwood Group arranged cover for
some 1600 schools, among them Eastbourne
College which suffered a serious fire in
November 1981.**

**Colin Ingleby-Mackenzie, Captain of
Hampshire county cricket team, Lords,
4 June 1958.**

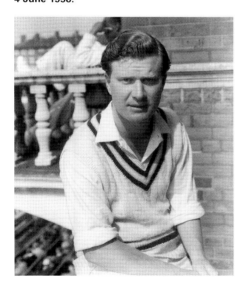

had eroded it substantially and made joining a larger company – in the event, Brown
Shipley – seem the best option. An interesting sideline came when Brown Shipley
helped its new subsidiary to purchase a Lloyd's broker called Wintle & Co. The pos-
sessions of this company included a battered black tin box filled with clanking metal
plaques that turned out to be a magnificent collection of firemarks, the earliest dating from the 17th century.

    With the break-up of the Brown Shipley Group in 1992, its entire Insurance divi-
sion, led by Colin Ingleby-Mackenzie, staged a management buyout. More than 50
members of staff invested personally in the equity of the new company, in partner-

ship with a venture capital firm, and thus the Holmwoods Group was born. Only a few years later, its management concluded that it would again fare better within a larger group. In 1995 it accepted an offer from Gibbs Hartley Cooper, and thus became a member of the HSBC Group.

While other classes of business were absorbed into existing divisions, the schools area became HSBC Gibbs Schools division, retaining much of its autonomy and virtually its entire staff. The range of institutions served at this time included some 1600 schools in the independent and grant-maintained sectors, including sixth-form colleges and technical colleges. Holmwoods was also the leading broker for accident and sickness contracts, and for personal accident insurance, where cover was provided for more than 750,000 pupils. A central office at Haywards Heath administered – as it does today – a country-wide network of account executives who can give the kind of individual attention schools require.

Fire marks have been in existence for over 300 years. Before the introduction of a house numbering system in the late 18th century, they signified which brigade was responsible for fighting the fire and which properties were insured, acting as an advertisement for the particular insurance company.

They are now a collectors' item, especially for those who worked in the insurance industry. These are three of the extensive collection of firemarks which Holmwoods acquired through Brown Shipley's purchase of Wintle and Co.

c. 1822. Hand in Hand Fire Office (founded in 1696). Ownership passed to Commercial Union in 1905. The clasped hands indicate friendship and unity. The number at the foot is the policy number.

c. 1824 West of Scotland Insurance Co, Glasgow. The crown depicted is an English crown represented heraldically and based on St Edwards crown made for the coronation of Charles II in 1662.

c.1795 Salamander was founded in 1790 and name changed to Wiltshire and Western in 1822. In 1835 it was amalgamated with Sun Fire, now part of Royal and Sun Alliance Group.

In Full Stride

By the mid-1990s Gibbs Hartley Cooper was once again competitive, due in part to more favourable conditions, but also to strong leadership at management level. The backing of HSBC had been invaluable in financing the new acquisitions and the search for the right executives, even if, at times, its innate conservatism had seemed to act as a brake on venturesome ideas. Gibbs Hartley Cooper's improved financial health is reflected in the variety of charts based on the balance sheets during this time, showing that gross revenues and profits all but trebled between 1990 and 1995.

In the latter year, for added coherence both within and outside the HSBC Group, the name of the company was changed to HSBC Gibbs. Traces of the Hartley Cooper identity remained: HSBC Gibbs (HCA), a leading specialist in the insurance needs of the fine art world and block insurances for the jewellery trade, was the

The improvement in revenues and profits between 1990 and 1993 are illustrated dramatically in the these graphs from HSBC Insurance Brokers' Summary Financial Report, 31 December 1993. The pie charts show the spread of the business.

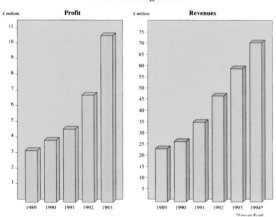

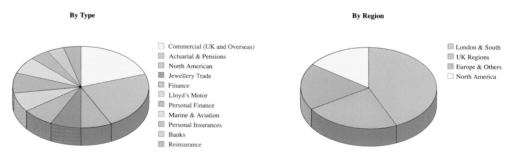

descendant of the Duveen & Walker of an earlier age, while the name of GHC Financial Institutions Insurance Services recalled the 85-year link with some of the world's largest banks in their fight against crime. But in general there was a gradual elimination of historical distinctions: Richards Longstaff was now known as the Estates division, and the former life and pensions business was now HSBC Gibbs Consulting, uniting the two main areas of benefit consultancy and financial planning. The emphasis was on integration and the steady rationalisation of how the company's somewhat complicated structure was presented to the insurance industry and to the public.

HSBC Gibbs Ltd was the holding entity for several separate companies dedicated to specific aspects of insurance broking. One of these was HSBC Gibbs Treaty Ltd (the former Treaty department) which was newly active in southern Europe, particularly in Italy. By 1997 it was generating one-seventh of HSBC Gibbs Ltd's overall income. Another was HSBC Gibbs North America Ltd, whose premium income had once been largely generated by the major independently owned brokers and managing agents in the United States: this was mainly non-marine business such as directors' and officers' liability, and medical malpractice. More recently, it had come to rely on the formation of specialist underwriting facilities for brokers in the U.S.A. and Canada. A third was HSBC Select, based at Newport in south Wales, which was one of the first professional telephone broking services. It had direct access to the marketplace and could advise on most types of personal insurance.

All of these entities except HSBC Select were based in London, at either Bishops Court or at Standard House, the former Gibbs headquarters. The company was also well represented abroad. HSBC Gibbs (Asia-Pacific) Ltd, located in Hong Kong, was a leading broker and risk consultant for corporate clients in the region, and was one of the larger brokers operating in Singapore. In the Middle East, HSBC Gibbs

The canopic bust above, from the 2008 *Tutankamun and the Golden Age of the Pharaohs* exhibition at the Dome, is one of the treasures covered by HSBC Insurance Brokers for prestigious clients. The specie practice arranges insurance for the worldwide needs of customers from the jewellery, fine art and antiques, museums and exhibitions and cash-in-transit sectors.

Marine business in Cyprus

In 1987 Wardley Cyprus (part of the HSBC Group) were in need of assistance to place insurance for a luxury yacht owned by one of the firm's large Cypriot banking clients. A representative of HSBC Insurance Brokers went to Cyprus to provide the necessary expertise and became aware of the possibilities for further marine-based insurance broking. Senior executives followed up with a fact-finding visit of their own, with the result that a manager was seconded to the Wardley Cyprus office for three months in September 1988 to test the waters. The exercise proved successful enough to warrant the decision to open a separate Cyprus branch in Limassol in March 1989, for offshore marine business.

Cyprus is well known in the maritime industry as a centre for shipmanagement companies, and one of the products which Cyprus branch developed for them was Errors and Omissions (E&O) indemnity. This type of insurance, arranged with International Transport Intermediaries Club Ltd, offered professional liability coverage against loss from a claim of alleged negligent acts, errors or omissions in the performance of professional services, and was not common amongst shipmanagers before. The branch also established the first insurance captive in Cyprus for an offshore shipmanager, and it was a founder member of the Cyprus Shipping Council and the Cyprus Offshore Enterprises Association.

HSBC Insurance Brokers' Cyprus branch has, in its turn, created business for other divisions: for example, the Construction division has developed business in Greece via a Cypriot construction client, and an onshore insurance broker has also been established to work with Group Insurance (Laiki) to win major local clients engaged in refinery and port business.

Cyprus is well known in the maritime industry as a centre for shipmanagement companies.

Osborne's Construction

Geoffrey Osborne, a civil engineer by profession, established Geoffrey Osborne Limited in March 1966. The company has grown into one of the U.K.'s leading family owned construction and civil engineering contractors, employing 1000 people and with a turnover of £251 million to 31 March 2007. Osborne operates from locations in the south-east and the Midlands, and its business is structured into seven operating divisions: Construction, Civil Engineering, Homes, Property Services, Rail, Development and Innovare.

The connection between Osborne and HSBC Insurance Brokers has its roots in Geoffrey Osborne's employment prior to setting up his own company. As former finance director David Burden, who took over responsibility for Osborne's insurance in 1969, relates: "Geoffrey had asked his previous employers, who were civil engineering contractors, if they could arrange cover for his new company through their insurance brokers. The brokers who put the cover in place were from a firm called Crawfurd Beck & Amos, which, through various mergers,

eventually became Holmwoods Insurance Brokers, and then part of HSBC's Gibbs Hartley Cooper in 1995."

Osborne's Construction division provides design and construction services for the education, health and property development sectors. The division works in partnership with N.H.S. trusts, local authorities and some of the country's leading colleges and universities to provide healthcare facilities, schools, further and higher educational establishments, office accommodation, and retail and industrial units. Osborne's excellence in construction was recognised recently with a Gold Award in the Chartered Institute of Building Construction Manager of the Year Awards for its work on the new science building for London Metropolitan University. The

The company has grown into one of the U.K.'s leading privately owned construction and civil engineering contractors, employing 1000 people.

firm is also due to complete the conversion of an Edwardian building at the London School of Economics in autumn 2008, enabling the world-class institution to more than double its teaching space.

Osborne's Civil Engineering division works on constructing and maintaining the U.K.'s road and rail network and on public infrastructure projects such as town centre regeneration and public parks. Recently completed projects include the new National Armed Forces Memorial in Staffordshire (shown opposite) opened by Her Majesty The Queen in October 2007.

Its Homes division is concerned with the development of environmentally friendly and sustainable communities and builds over 500 affordable homes, including care homes, every year, including the 180-home Queensbridge Development in Peckham, London, completed in summer 2007.

Osborne's Property Services division provides responsive repairs and planned maintenance to over 40,000 housing association homes in the south-east, and maintains railway buildings and structures for a number of leading train-operating companies.

In all HSBC Insurance Brokers has now been arranging insurance cover for Osborne for over 40 years.

A very modern motorway

The Attiki Odos, known also as Attica Tollway or Athens Peripherique, is a 65 km toll motorway serving the greater metropolitan area of Athens. Timed for the Athens Olympics in 2004, this was a pioneering project in terms of how it was funded, the fact that it is a closed toll motorway operated by a concessionaire, and its in-built safety factors. The project came about as a result of the Greek government conducting an international tender to build the road, which stipulated co-financing and the creation of a single entity to undertake the work and operate and maintain the road on completion of construction. The consortium that won the tender is called Attiki Odos S.A.

The construction work was completed on time and within Attiki Odos S.A.'s planned budget of approximately €1.3 billion, which was financed by the Greek government, the European Union and equity invested by Attiki Odos S.A. itself, and through loans arranged by an international banking group on a project finance basis.

The motorway consists of two main highways: the Elefsina Stavros Spata motorway (52 km) and the Imittos Western Peripheral motorway (13 km), together forming a backbone linking all transport of Attica – road, rail, airport and ports. There is also a special traffic island for the operation of the suburban railway built in parallel with the road. The construction of the road adhered to strict safety-related specifications, which included hard shoulders in both directions, a central traffic island, skid-resistant asphalt surfaces of high durability, dense lighting and fencing. As part of the contract, Attiki Odos S.A. were required to ensure that traffic flowed smoothly and safely at all times: to achieve this,

Timed for the Athens Olympics in 2004, this was a pioneering project in terms of how it was funded.

special control cameras linked to a
traffic management centre were built in
all along the length of the road to ensure
continual monitoring of traffic on a
24-hour-a-day basis.

It is also Attiki Odos S.A.'s
responsibility to operate the motorway
and maintain it: it funds this by applying
tolls, charging a flat rate to encourage
longer journeys but varying the cost
according to the vehicle class, while
discounts are given for vehicles
equipped with an electronic transponder.
Operation is undertaken by Attikes
Diadromes S.A., an entity which is
regarded in the international arena as a
very reputable operator, winning the first
prize in the European Road Safety Award
established by the International Road
Federation for its traffic safety practices.

HSBC Insurance Brokers has worked
for Attiki Odos S.A., and with their
independent advisor Antonis Gavrilis,
since 1997. They were involved in
advising on insurance issues throughout
the finance negotiation period and then in
placing the insurance programme through
the construction phase. On completion of
the motorway, HSBC Insurance Brokers
also placed the insurance for Attiki Odos
S.A.'s operational risks.

was also one of the largest brokers. It had operated in Dubai since 1975, where its clients included both local businesses and the resident branches of major international companies; and in Oman since 1976, where it acted as an advisor to local governmental and commercial organisations and created pension schemes for the Royal Omani Police and the Royal Guard of Oman. For a time there was also an office in Saudi Arabia. Since 1989 HSBC Gibbs had been active in Cyprus, providing specialist insurance services to the maritime industries there. As the only Lloyd's broker on the island, it had also come to offer a full range of corporate insurance

A presentation of a pension scheme for the Royal Omani Police and the Royal Guard of Oman, on which HSBC Gibbs advised local government and commercial organisations.

The *Ramform Sovereign*, the latest and largest of a series of seismic survey vessels insured through HSBC Insurance Brokers' energy practice.

services. Offices in Bermuda, India, Dublin and Chicago (the last two were closed in 2000) acted as links with local insurers, or as local facilitators of business in their respective geographical spheres.

In 1999 the name of HSBC Gibbs was changed to HSBC Insurance Brokers Limited, and the last overt reference to the company's long history disappeared. Did this provoke a pang of nostalgia? If so, perhaps only momentarily. The benefits of being part of the HSBC Group were by this time simply too overwhelming. Its backing over the previous 15 years had enabled its insurance arm to weather hard times for the sector, to make essential acquisitions, to expand its portfolio and, in the case of some specialist areas, to buy in much needed expertise. Membership of the HSBC Group gave access to the international network of one of the world's largest banking

The Grace Spitfire, ML407, survived 176 World War II flying missions. Restored by Nick Grace, it flew again in 1985. Since his death in 1988, his wife Carolyn has flown the historic aeroplane, to the delight of audiences around the U.K. HSBC Insurance has sponsored the Grace Spitfire insurance since 2006.

and financial services organisations. Whether directly – in the provision of advice and services in such areas as trade finance, cash and investment management, treasury and foreign exchange – or indirectly, through processing services backed by information technology, financial controls and disciplines, such relationships worked in the interest of clients, and hence, overall, in that of the company.

By 2001 HSBC Insurance Brokers had seen its revenue climb to £148 million (from £66.5 million in 1995) and its pre-tax profits increase to £26.5 million (from £8.5 million in 1995). The profitability in 2001 was enhanced by the insurance market's reaction to the terrorist attacks which took place in the U.S.A. on 11 September 2001, whereby premium rates were substantially increased across all classes of businesses, ending nearly a decade of "soft" insurance markets. More problematic for HSBC's Insurance Brokers was the fact that the insurance companies significantly reduced their capacity and became unwilling to offer renewal terms for clients with bad claim histories. This was a testing time for the broking staff, yet it also gave them an opportunity to demonstrate to their clients that they were able to place insurance despite such obstacles.

Given HSBC's origins in Hong Kong and Shanghai, it is fitting that its next significant venture heralded its return to China. Beijing HSBC Insurance Brokers was formed in 2003 with 24.9 per cent of the equity in conjunction with a Chinese partner. Offices were also opened in Shanghai and Guangzhou and the business in all three has increased rapidly, benefiting from the huge expansion of the Chinese economy. HSBC Insurance Brokers increased its shareholding to 95 per cent in June 2008.

Relatively benign trading conditions prevailed in 2002 and 2003. However, the world of insurance broking encountered a new challenge in late 2004 when Elliot Spitzer, the attorney general of New York State, accused the three largest firms of

The Falkland Islands

In December 2007 HSBC Insurance Brokers' Birmingham office celebrated the 20th anniversary of its association with the Falkland Islands government. The Islands cover an area similar in extent to Wales but it has a population of around 2400 people, the majority of whom live in the capital, Stanley. The economy of the Islands was traditionally based on sheep ranching, though it has now been developed to include tourism from the cruise ships which regularly stop there.

HSBC Insurance Brokers initially became involved with the Falkland Islands government when an entrepreneurial sales executive in the Birmingham office came across a public invitation to tender for the provision of insurances and decided to respond. After securing the business, it was subsequently discovered that HSBC Insurance Brokers had been the only brokers to respond!

The services which HSBC Insurance Brokers' provided included risk management and insurance advice in a host of different areas ranging from health and social services, police, public works, schools, power generation, airports, floating harbours and coastal shipping. Providing service on a daily basis to a major client 8000 miles and a four hour time difference away was not something that many other brokers were eager to take up, but for HSBC Insurance Brokers, it was a challenge for which tailor-made solutions were found, which included a yearly visit to review exposure risks. Of course, communication is now made very much easier with the development of new communication technology.

The Islands cover an area similar in extent to Wales but it has a population of around 2400 people.

The Berkeley Group

The Berkeley Group was founded in 1976, initially concentrating on the construction of single homes and executive developments. The business grew very rapidly, and in December 1985 the group gained a full listing on the London Stock Exchange.

During the early 1990s, the group decided to focus its skills and expertise on complex brownfield sites in towns and cities and it acquired a reputation for its innovative approach to urban regeneration, focusing on mixed-use developments and the creation of sustainable communities. The group's philosophy is to devolve operational responsibility and accountability to autonomous management teams. As a result, its principal divisions, Berkeley Homes, St George and St James, have all established strong brand identities. Creating partnerships is a key part of the way in which the Berkeley Group works and it has undertaken joint ventures with a number of companies including Land Securities, Thames Water and, more recently, Prudential. The group also works in partnership with a number of local authorities to regenerate areas of London and the south-east of England.

Today, the Berkeley Group is firmly established as a market leader in urban regeneration.

HSBC Insurance Brokers tendered for the Berkeley Group's insurance programme in 2003. Their considerable experience in being able to provide insurance solutions to individual enterprises was a key factor in winning the tender and they continue to arrange insurance for the group today. The range of cover required is wide and HSBC Insurance Brokers restructured the group's insurance programme to suit the activities of the business, ranging from small 30-unit schemes to large mixed-use urban regeneration schemes which can take ten to fifteen years to complete. The Berkeley Group requires relationships that both add value to its business and share common business philosophies – such as short lines of communication and an attention to detail – and the group believes that this is what continues to differentiate HSBC Insurance Brokers from its competitors.

The range of cover required is wide and HSBC Insurance Brokers restructured Berkeley's insurance programme.

Three specific examples of schemes where the Berkeley Group and HSBC Insurance Brokers have worked together are Imperial Wharf, London (St George); Royal Arsenal, Woolwich (Berkeley Homes); and Gunwharf Quays, Portsmouth Harbour (Berkeley Homes).

Imperial Wharf is a new riverside community built on 13 hectares of previously neglected and derelict waterfront space alongside the river Thames in Fulham. The development comprises 1800 homes, 28,000 sq m of commercial space, including cafés, bars and restaurants, and a 4-hectare park.

The Royal Arsenal site in south-east London is a 31-hectare site which exemplifies mixed-use urban regeneration and forms part of the entire regeneration of a historic riverside location. The site was in its time Britain's largest and most important centre for manufacturing military equipment and munitions, and some of the buildings date back to the 17th century. Many of the historic buildings have been restored, including 18 listed buildings, and the Berkeley Group has worked alongside a number of organisations, including English Heritage, the Woolwich Historical Society, the Conservation Office and the Environment Agency, to ensure that the

Imperial Wharf

Royal Arsenal remains faithful to its historical past. Once complete, it will provide over 3750 homes.

Gunwharf Quays at Portsmouth Harbour is based on one of Britain's most historic naval dockyards. Its development was part of a much-needed regeneration programme for Portsmouth and it has now become a landmark waterfront location. It is a mixed-use development, and includes 900 homes (including a 30-storey landmark tower at the centre of the scheme), 44,000 sq m of commercial space, including a 130-bed hotel, and some 2800 sq m of office space. The site has won many awards, including the BURA Crystal Award for Best Practice in Regeneration in 2005, for being one of the best of its previous winners.

insurance brokers of practices which he considered unethical, including receiving "contingent commissions", which he required them to stop accepting immediately. The effect on HSBC Insurance Brokers was minimal initially, because the company was not large enough to generate significant contingent commissions. However, the three largest brokers reacted during 2005 and 2006 by attempting to fill the resulting gap in their revenue through aggressive fee reductions to win new clients. This effect was exacerbated by the return of a "soft" insurance market and the strengthening US dollar, which significantly reduced the profitability of HSBC Insurance Brokers.

By 2007 it had become clear that HSBC Insurance Brokers had to take action to combat the challenging market conditions and, accordingly, in the second half of 2007 the business was restructured. The most noticeable effect was that the servicing of the firm's commercial clients moved from the regional offices into the Bournemouth office, in order to improve client service and reduce costs. At the same time a significant investment was allocated to redesign procedures and to invest in technology to achieve straight-through processing to improve client service. A particular feature of this, which will change for ever the traditional paper strewn office of a typical insurance broker, is the introduction of electronic document imaging. The company has also reorganised its sales force and recruited new business developers.

Following the reorganisation, HSBC Insurance Brokers now comprises six main client groupings: Commercial, Corporate, Specialty, Complex Risks, Wholesale and Overseas. Commercial is aimed at clients paying insurance premiums up to £75,000 who are serviced predominantly by telephone and internet from the Bournemouth office. These clients have mainly been introduced to HSBC Insurance Brokers by HSBC Bank, often through its sales staff located in the bank's commercial banking centres. Corporate broking looks after the larger clients with insurance premiums above £75,000 from the UK regional offices. These clients require a sophisticated risk management service and often need an individually tailored insurance programme. Specialty areas include Education, Estates, Private Clients, Professional Indemnity and Trade Credit businesses, all of whom have client service delivery requirements that are different from mainstream commercial and corporate businesses. Complex Risks comprises the Lloyd's and London Market Practices that provide industry-specific solutions and are provided directly to clients around the world. This also includes the specialist practice offices in Cyprus and Germany. Wholesale activity differs from the other customer groupings because it provides a service to other brokers, either smaller brokers in the U.K. who need the company's assistance

A current member of staff, at Vintners' Place, using the new electronic document system.

to find competitive prices, or brokers elsewhere in the world that need to access the Lloyd's or the London market for price or coverage reasons. Overseas covers the corporate broking activities located in some of the fastest growing economies in the world: Abu Dhabi, China, Dubai, Hong Kong, India, Qatar, Saudi Arabia, Singapore, South Korea, Taiwan, and Vietnam.

A consistent theme throughout HSBC Insurance Broker's 200-year history has been its ability to be flexible and responsive to changing market and client needs. It has grown from small beginnings at the time of the Napoleonic Wars to being able to offer its clients the full range of specialised services expected from an international insurance broker and risk management advisor in the age of the internet. In 2007 HSBC Insurance Brokers was arguably the fifth largest international broker operating in the U.K. market. Its positioning in the insurance broking market is that it provides the "intelligent alternative" to the largest international brokers that dominate the market. The firm's appeal is to clients who demand a personalised service from knowledgeable staff, rather than the standardised offering available from many of its competitors. This appeal is backed up by the financial strength and brand awareness of the HSBC Group together with HSBC's desire to grow insurance activities to become a significant profit generator for the Group.

As HSBC Insurance Brokers moves into its third century, the history of the last 200 years provides a base from which it can look forward. The attributes that have contributed to the firm's past success – excellent client service, a high quality and dedicated staff, and the flexibility to adapt to changing markets and client needs – will stand the business in good stead for a successful future.

Appendices

Appendix 1: Select Bibliography

The principal source for the history of Antony Gibbs & Sons Limited was the extensive collection of papers relating to the firm housed at the Guildhall Library, London. For Hartley Cooper, and for the various companies that have become part of HSBC Insurance Brokers over the years, there exists very little in the way of primary material. A miscellaneous collection of documents, annual reports, brochures and house magazines has been supplemented by interviews with a number of retired senior figures. Of the secondary works consulted, the following have provided factual information and helpful insights.

Blakemore, Harold, *From the Pacific to La Paz. The Antofagasta and Bolivia Railway Company 1888-1988*. London, 1990.

Brown, Antony, *Greig Fester. A story of Reinsurance*. Cambridge, 1996.

Budelman, Robert B. and Webb, Joseph R.A., *Safe Deposit Boxes. Dealing With Losses*. London, 1981.

Cameron, Alan and Farndon, Roy, *Scenes from Sea and City. Lloyd's List 1734-1984*. Lloyd's List 250th Anniversary Special Supplement. London, 1984.

Chapman, Stanley, *Merchant Enterprise in Britain. From the Industrial Revolution to World War I*. Cambridge, 1992.

Chapman, Stanley, *The Rise of Merchant Banking*. London 1984.

Crocker, William Charles, *Tales from the Coffee House. Stories about Lloyd's*. Plymouth, 1973.

Gibbs, J. A., *The History of Antony and Dorothea Gibbs & of the Early Years of Antony Gibbs & Sons*. London, 1922.

Gunn, Cathy, *Nightmare on Lime Street. Whatever Happened to Lloyd's of London?* London, 1992.

Jones, Colin, *Antony Gibbs & Sons Limited. A Record of 150 Years of Merchant Banking 1808-1958*. London, 1958.

King, Frank H. H., *The History of the Hong Kong and Shanghai Banking Corporation. Volume IV. The Hong Kong Bank in the Period of Development and Nationalism, 1941-1984. From Regional Bank to Multinational Group*. Cambridge, 1991.

Mathew, W.M., *The House of Gibbs and the Peruvian Guano Monopoly*. London, 1981.

Mathew, W. M., "Peru and the British Guano Market, 1840-1870". *Economic History Review (2nd series), vol. 23:1 (1970), pp. 112-128*.

Maude, Wilfred, *Antony Gibbs & Sons Ltd., Merchants and Bankers 1808-1958*. London, 1958.

Mayo, John, "British Commission Houses and the Chilean Economy 1850-80". *Journal of Latin American Studies XI* (1979).

Platt, D. C. M., *Business Imperialism 1840-1930. An inquiry based on British experience in Latin America*. Oxford, 1977.

Roberts, Richard, *Schroders. Merchants & Bankers*. London 1992.

Sharman, Sarah, *Sir James Martin*. Yeovil, 1996.

Twitchett, John, *Lloyd's and the Banks*. London, 1991

Wines, Richard A., *Fertiliser in America. From waste recycling to resource exploitation*. Philadelphia, 1985.

Wright, Charles, and Fayle, C. Ernest, *A History of Lloyd's from the founding of Lloyd's coffee-house to the present day*. London, 1928.

Appendix 2: List of Chairmen since 1900

HARTLEY COOPER

E.E. Cooper	1900
Col. Sir S. Wishart	1922
C.R. Bland	1935
R.H. Lindley	1939
R.E. Fawcus	1940
F.C. Callow	1953
J.G. East	1963
T.R. Bland	1974
J.P.F. Ive	1977
E. Norris	1980
J.E. Jewiss	1982

GIBBS

Lord Cullen of Ashbourne	1931	
Hon. Sir Geoffrey C. Gibbs KCMG	1932	
Sir David Gibbs	1964	
T.M. Gauge	1968	
W.D. Robson	1983	*Hartley Cooper and Gibbs merge*
J.R. Millner	1984	*Becomes Gibbs Hartley Cooper*
G.F. Puttergill	1985	*Name changed to HSBC Gibbs in 1997*
A.P. Hope	2000	*1999 HSBC Gibbs becomes HSBC Insurance Brokers*
S.G. Troop	2006	
C. Schnor	2007	

| 1800 | 1810 | 1820 | 1830 | 1840 | 1850 | 1860 | 1870 | 1880 | 1890 | 1900 |

1808
Antony Gibbs & Sons incorporated
as merchant bank

1843
James Hartley and Co. (Steamship
Brokers) incorporated

Appendix 3: HSBC Insurance Brokers timeline

1874
E.E. Cooper and Co. established

1900
James Hartley Cooper
formed following merger

1865
Hongkong and Shanghai Banking Corporation founded

1840 C. Holmwood

1889 Bank of Bermuda

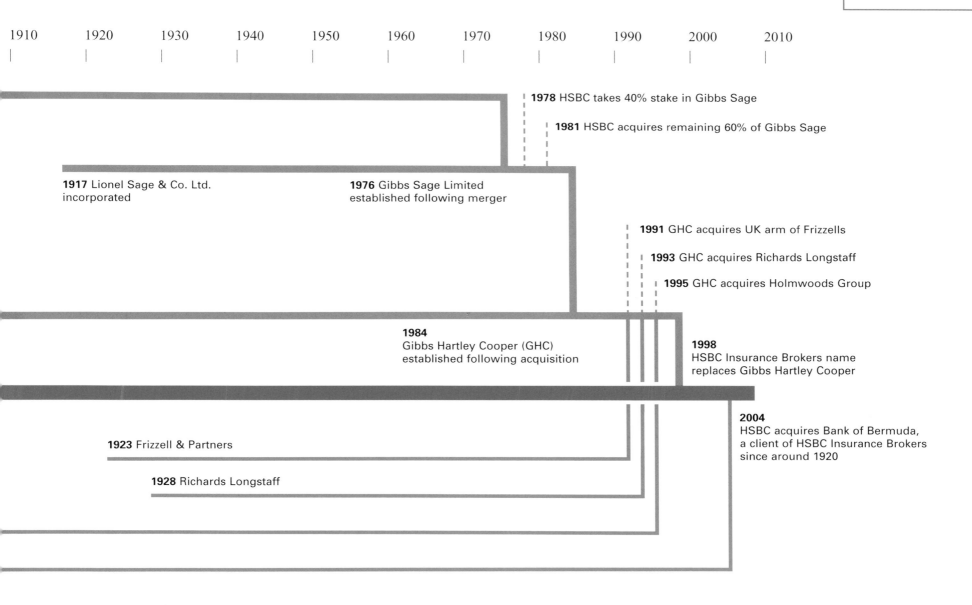

1910   1920   1930   1940   1950   1960   1970   1980   1990   2000   2010

1978 HSBC takes 40% stake in Gibbs Sage

1981 HSBC acquires remaining 60% of Gibbs Sage

1917 Lionel Sage & Co. Ltd.
incorporated

1976 Gibbs Sage Limited
established following merger

1991 GHC acquires UK arm of Frizzells

1993 GHC acquires Richards Longstaff

1995 GHC acquires Holmwoods Group

1984
Gibbs Hartley Cooper (GHC)
established following acquisition

1998
HSBC Insurance Brokers name
replaces Gibbs Hartley Cooper

1923 Frizzell & Partners

2004
HSBC acquires Bank of Bermuda,
a client of HSBC Insurance Brokers
since around 1920

1928 Richards Longstaff

Appendix 4: Glossary of General Insurance Terms

Addendum An amendment to a Cover Note or other document

Assured (or Insured) The person or company in whose name the insurance is arranged

Assurers (or Insurers or Underwriters or Security) The insurance companies or underwriters who undertake the risk in a policy of insurance

Brokerage (or Commission) The percentage of premium allowed by Insurers to the Broker as remuneration for the work involved in placing the insurance. Paid by the Insured as part of the Gross Premium

Binding Authority An insurance contract wherein the Underwriter(s) delegates his underwriting authority to another (the Coverholder). Risks may be bound (placed on cover) and Certificates issued within set limits and conditions without reference to the underwriter

Bordereau(x) Usually a list of Declarations against a Binding Authority or Lineslip for a given period i.e. monthly, quarterly showing, inter alia, premiums or claims due for settlement

Cedant An Insurer who passes (cedes) part of the risk he has underwritten to another underwriter known as a Reinsurer

Certificate Evidence of cover issued in lieu of a policy document

Claim Advice of a loss under a policy of insurance

Clause An attachment to a policy of insurance (usually printed) containing a condition of that insurance

Closing A document addressed to the Underwriter containing details of the premium due or claim collection

Collecting Commission A marine term for a payment made to the broker by the client or the underwriter for work undertaken in claim collections

Coinsurer (or Coinsuring Companies) Other Insurers subscribing to the policy of insurance

Commission 1. Brokerage

2. A payment made to a third party, say, for introducing or producing the business

Cover Note A document provided as evidence of cover pending issuance of the policy document

Debit Note (or Invoice) A bill for the insurance premium

Declaration A risk attaching to a Binding Authority or Lineslip or Cover Lineslip

Deductible An amount borne by the Assured and deducted from the claim payment. See Excess

Discount 1. Slip Discount – the total brokerage and commission allowed by underwriters.
2. Client Discount – the reduction in the gross premium allowed by the Broker to the Client
3. Other e.g. Prompt Payment Discount – the discount allowed by the underwriter to the Assured for prompt payment of the premium

Endorsement A written or printed document evidencing an alteration to the insurance policy or slip

Excess The amount above which underwriters are liable in the event of a claim. See also Deductible

Exclusion Property or peril not covered by the insurance policy

Fronting A 100% Reinsurance arrangement whereby the underwriter issuing the original policy is said to 'front' for the Reinsurers who are the 'true' underwriters. E.g. an underwriter may not be licensed to write business in a particular country so the broker selects an underwriter who is licenced to 'front' for the one that is not

Hazard (or Peril) The risk which is being insured against e.g. fire, burglary etc

Honeycomb Endorsement An endorsement to a London market Slip facilitating underwriters' agreement to a change in the original slip details or terms and conditions

Information Details concerning the risk which may or may not be included in the policy document

Insurance (or Assurance)	A contract or agreement whereby an eventuality or Risk may be guarded against by payment of a premium. (The term Assurance is usually applied to life business)
Insurer	The entity accepting (underwriting) the risk. See Underwriter
Interest	A term applied to the property or liability insured e.g. Stock or Employers Liability
IUA (International Underwriting Assoc)	An entity established to represent the insurance companies within the London insurance market and to provide central processing facilities on behalf of those companies
Layer	A large insurance risk may be placed in several stages or layers, the first layer meeting claims 'from the ground up' to a specified limit; the second paying claims when the first layer is exhausted etc
Licenced underwriters	Underwriters who are licenced by law to underwrite business in a particular country
Limit (of liability)	The maximum amount payable by the underwriter to the insured under and insurance policy
Line	1. Written Line – the amount, usually a percentage, accepted by an underwriter on a given risk 2. Signed Line – where a policy is over subscribed the calculated percentage applicable to the underwriter
Lineslip	An insurance facility whereby a market is established by the broker for a book of business and Declarations against that lineslip are agreed by the leading underwriter(s) only on behalf of the following or remaining underwriters
Lloyd's	A market comprising groups of Syndicates formed to underwrite insurance risks
Loss	The occurrence of an insured event giving rise to a claim under the insurance policy
Long Term Agreement	An undertaking by an assured to offer renewal of an insurance in consideration of which a reduced premium is charged
Period	The length of time for which the insurance policy is effected
Policy	The formal legal document evidencing the contract of insurance
Premium	The money (or consideration) paid by the Assured to the Underwriters for the insurance policy
Proposal (Form)	An application form for the insurance containing information about the Assured and Risk
Rate	The basis for calculating the premium
Reinsurance	The 'laying-off' or ceding of part of a risk from one underwriter to another. Types of Reinsurance are: 1. Excess of Loss 2. Proportional Treaty
Reinsurer	The underwriter who accepts the 'laid-off' element of the risk
Retention	When a reinsurance is effected the retention is that part of the risk retained by the original underwriter
Settlement Due Date	For London market business, the date by which the underwriter expects the premium to be paid
Situation (Location)	The physical location of the risk
Slip	For business placed in the London insurance market, a document Brokers uses to place the insurance. The Slip contains the details, terms and conditions of the risk and policy
Subscription policy	A single policy signed by all underwriters
Sum Insured	The amount of risk insured under the policy
Surplus Line	Underwriters who are approved by the relevant Underwriters insurance authorities to underwrite business which cannot be placed with local or licenced underwriters (such as in the USA)
Terms	Part of the conditions of a Slip or Policy
Underwriter	The Insurer accepting the risk or part thereof. Currently one or more of: 1. Lloyd's syndicate 2. Insurance Company
Warranty	A condition which must be complied with. Failure to do so will allow underwriters to void the policy entirely
Warranty company	An insurance company who participates in a policy and whom other underwriters agree to follow so far as terms and claims are concerned
Wording	An attachment to the printed policy setting out terms and conditions etc.

Appendix 5: The Marine Broking Process in use until the Early 1970s

Enquiries

Enquiries for Insurances to be placed into the Lloyd's of London market came from two main sources: Direct from the Assured i.e. a UK based shipowner requiring marine insurance or via a Producing Broker (or Intermediary) e.g. D.K. Ludwig (National Bulk Carriers) in the U.S.A requiring marine insurance for his 70 strong fleet of ships would approach a U.S broker such as Marsh & McLennan who in turn would request Hartley Cooper & Co. to obtain terms from the London market.

Communication

In the 1950's and 1960's the main method of communicating sufficient data for a quotation was via letter (air mail, 3 days to USA). Cables (similar to inland telegrams) were used for urgent overnight communication and consisted of a few lines only. A Cable received in the morning required a response that evening even if only "Working, will revert", whereas a letter's response was deemed satisfactory if the reply was made within 7 days. The 1970's and 1980's saw the advent of telex then fax which once developed properly made a significant difference to communication generally.

Risk presentation

Upon receipt of details of the risk to be insured whether it be vessel value, age, type, classification, size etc., or description of the shipyard operation, turnover, payroll, type of work undertaken etc. for a ship repairer's liability, the information would need to presented in a format suitable for the insurance market.

The document that contained this information was called a "slip" and consisted of a thin card folded concertina fashion upon which were typed details such as Insurance Type (e.g. Hull & Machinery); Form (e.g. S.G., the main marine policy form). Other details such as Assured, Period of Insurance, Insurable Interest, Value & Sum Insured, Navigating Warranties, Conditions of Insurance (additional to the marine perils stated in the SG form), Deductibles (Excesses), Premium, Deductions (Broker's Commission), Other Material Information such as claims record.

Usually the slip would be drafted by an insurance technician or the broker himself.

Broking process

The broker would take the slip(s) to the market either to obtain quotations or for placing.

Typically, a marine risk would be offered to a "Leading Underwriter" for an indication of the likely premium and other terms and conditions. The broker would solicit support for those terms and conditions from "Following Underwriters" until he was confident that he could obtain 100% support if the client accepted the quote.

Brokers were expected to be in the market all day and not return to the office until late afternoon. They would then translate their quotes into a letter or brief cable for despatch to the client (Assured or Intermediary).

Upon acceptance of the quoted premium, terms and conditions, the details would be re-typed onto another slip called the "Placing Slip" and the broker would then obtain each Underwriter's formal stamp and initials and percentage or amount of the risk they were prepared to underwrite. This would continue until such time as the slip had a minimum of 100% or the amount of the Sum Insured. Over subscription was normal London market practice and the percentages or amounts would be reduced to the required 100% or amount.

Once an Underwriter had "committed" his line, effectively he was on risk for that amount of liability. The slip itself was not a legal document as the policy was evidence of the contract, but could be used as evidence in litigation.

The broker or technician would then communicate to the client that the risk had been placed successfully.

Pre Policy Documentation

Having placed the risk, typically a Cover Note would be produced. This was a retyping of the slip terms and conditions, expanded where necessary for clarity and detailing the Underwriters names and share of the risk. This was necessary because of the time taken to produce and "sign" the policy document(s).

Additionally, a "Debit Note" (Invoice) would be typed detailing the amount of premium due from the client.

Note that Gross Premium quoted by the Underwriters included the broker's Commission i.e. the remuneration allowed by the Underwriters for placing the business.

Insurance Policy

To facilitate the signing of the policy(ies) and "taking down" (settlement) of the premium to underwriters, a Signing Slip would be typed mirroring the Placing Slip together with the individual Lloyd's Syndicate proportions.

The formal Lloyd's (and I.L.U. (Institute of London Underwriters, if marine insurance companies were involved) policy document(s) would be prepared by the Lloyd's Broker. The usual policy forms would be S.G. (Ship & Goods) supplemented by the relevant Institute Time Clauses and other clauses as specified in the slip.

In the 1950's and 1960's formal credit terms did not exist between brokers and underwriters or brokers and clients. The broker debited the client with the premium and was paid in due course. The broker submitted the policy and a "closing" document to the L.P.S.O (Lloyd's Policy Signing Office) which was the central policy checking/signing "bureau". Likewise for the I.L.U.. Premium settlement to underwriters via central settlement took place a month later.

Each policy document, and there may have been multiple copies, would have been produced on a typewriter. Policies then still carried a 6d stamp duty. Any additional wording would have been produced using a wax stencil and duplicated using a Roneo or Gestetner duplicating machine. Wording and clauses would be attached inside the policy form using sellotape.

Once the policy was checked by LPSO staff it would be allocated a Signing Date & Number which would be stamped on both policy and signing slip. Usually Lloyd's policies would be submitted first then the ILU. The whole process taking up to 3 months.

When signed the original (1st copy) policies would either be retained in the office for safe keeping and potential claims use and a copy sent to the client or the original despatched to the client.

Claims

Typically claims would be handled by the same broking house that placed the risk. The client would notify the broker of a potential claim and the broker would put underwriters on notice and obtain further instructions such as surveyor, loss adjuster etc..

On potentially contentious claims the broker's skill in negotiating a satisfactory settlement was invaluable.

On marine risks, a Collecting Commission was payable, usually 1% of the claim value. This was an insurable interest and the Assured could effect an insurance policy accordingly. This was Market practice in those days, but unusual today.

As with premium settlement, the claims documentation would be attached to the original policy and submitted for "taking down" and collection from underwriters in due course.

Appendix 6: Relative purchasing power of a '2008 £1'

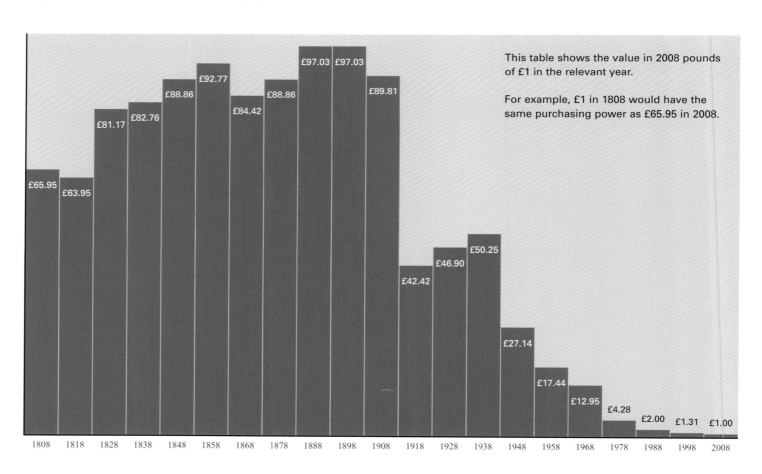

This table shows the value in 2008 pounds of £1 in the relevant year.

For example, £1 in 1808 would have the same purchasing power as £65.95 in 2008.

Appendix 7: Acknowledgements

Our grateful thanks for help, information and advice to:-

Peter Ahlas	George Francis	Bill Rainbow
Lord Aldenham	Colin Frizzell	Carol Ranger
John Barnett	David Godfray	Brian Richardson
Tony Barratt	Philip Gregory	David Robson
Tom Bland	Malcolm Grint	Mike Rusby
John Bovington (d. 2008)	Tony Hope	Mary Shaw
Ron Brazier	Simon Howell	Geoffrey Shepheard
David Coppin	Keith Jones	Geoff Sherman
Peter de Pinna	Sara Kinsey	Morley Speed
Les Durrant	Phil Lazell	Tina Staples
Chris East	Bob Murrell	June Trevett
John East (d. 2007)	Peter Newnham	Ray Winch
Norman Epps	Eddie Norris	
Steve Flowers	Graham Puttergill	

Project managers Tim Kemp and Charles Ledsam would also like to express their appreciation to clients, underwriters and all those who gave their help in producing this history. Grateful thanks are due to Jo'e Coleby, Peter Dolton and Tony Littlechild of Book Production Consultants for their assistance in the production of this book.

Illustrations are from the collections of HSBC Insurance Brokers Ltd, except for the following, reproduced by kind permission of:

AEG Nikolaus & Co., p. 108; *Antony Gibbs & Sons Ltd, Merchants and Bankers 1808-1968* by W. Maude; p. 1, p. 3, p. 10 (bottom), p. 22, p. 39; Attiki Odos, pp. 112-113; J. Baikie, p. 103; Bateman Archives; p. 25, p. 60 (top); Berkeley Group, p. 118-119; Corbis; p. 9, p. 81, p. 98, p. 117; Laurie Dennett; p. 11; Exchem, pp. 100-101; *Fertile Fortune: The Story of Tyntesfield* by James Miller; p. 1, p. 10 (top); Mr G. Francis, p. 67; Getty Images, p. 76 (top), p. 77; Mr M. Grint, p. 60 (bottom); Darren Harbar, p. 115; Imperial War Museum; p. 23, p. 62; Lloyd's Archives; p. 4, p. 5, p. 39, p. 54, p. 57, p. 66, p. 68 (top), p. 69, p. 73; Martin - Baker, pp. 70-71; Mary Evans Picture Library; p. 7, p. 15, p. 18, pp. 20-21, p. 41; Mornflake Archives, pp. 36-37; Motor Picture Library, p. 76 (bottom); National Trust Picture Library; p. 1, p. 12; *One Hundred Years without a course: a History of Lloyd's Golf Club*, by B. Evens, p. 47; Osborne Construction, pp. 110-111; David Robson, p. 33; Mary Shaw, p. 64; Judy Slinn, pp. 30-31; S.S. *Great Britain* Trust; p. 6; Mr R. Stormonth Darling, p. 85, p. 105; Mr C. Webb, p. 80; Mr R. Winch, p. 114 (top).

Every effort has been made to obtain permission for the reproduction of the illustrations and photographs in the book; apologies are offered to anyone whom it has not been possible to contact.

The publishers would like to thank Mr Alan Brown, Lloyd's Archivist for his invaluable assistance with the illustrations for this project and Mitzi de Margary for her photography on behalf of HSBC Insurance Brokers Ltd.

Index of companies